Ascent of Woman

Ascent of Woman

ELISABETH MANN BORGESE

George Braziller · *New York* · *1963*

Contents

Ascent of Woman

PROLOGUE

Credo - Vedo

Pessimism is the result of incomplete knowledge or of too short a view. Any general or long-run pessimism is contradicted by the facts of evolution and progress in the past.

JULIAN HUXLEY[1]

Credo: I am a liberal, a progressive, and an optimist. I believe that men and women are born with equal rights and equal possibilities.

Vedo: A liberal, progressive, and optimistic society has granted them equal rights. But they are not born with equal possibilities. No law has been able to confer these on them. It is still a man's world.

Credo: It's because women have not yet been given a chance. Their emancipation is of recent date and far from complete. Millennia of subjection weigh on them.

Vedo: In the long run people get what they deserve. Women's millennial subjection can be explained only by their relative inferiority.

Credo: No, no, and no. True, I have no explanation for the fact of woman's subjection, *la chute,* except for her physical weakness, which once mattered . . .

Vedo: You are begging the question.

Credo: . . . but does not matter today. I know, on the other hand, that the state of subjection, once established, has acted on woman's mind and body. Most of her so-called secondary sex characters are not natural but nurtural.

Vedo: Most, perhaps. Not all, certainly. I see that women bear the brunt of procreation. And no matter how one tries to reduce their burden, it's a handicap. Not even a hundred years of emancipation have been able to overcome it.

Credo: In a free world, in a civilized world, a woman is free to reject the burden of procreation. She can choose between

3

       motherhood and greatness in work, art, science, and
       saintliness.

Vedo: The very choice—not imposed on men, who can be
       fathers and great, but only on women—is an injustice,
       an act of discrimination, a handicap. Men start the race
       for greatness from a point of advantage. No getting
       away from it. And they are taller. And they are
       stronger; their blood is richer in red corpuscles; their
       brain weight, greater; their reactions, prompter. No get-
       ting away from it. And the results of their efforts cor-
       roborate the statement. Just look at the record.

Credo: If I am a woman—an artist, perhaps, and sensitive—
       deep down I feel that there is something in what you
       say. Yet my reason refuses to accept it. I am unable to
       accept the consequences logically inherent in your point
       of view. For if women were indeed inferior, or at least
       handicapped by nature, how could they justify their
       claim to equal rights?

Vedo: By appealing to men's chivalry; by appealing to men's
       charity.

Credo: No, no, and no. I, for one, don't want equal rights if I
       know that I cannot offer equal work in return.

Vedo: The fighting type of women's-righters have always
       struck me as tragicomic.

Credo: What you see, reactionaries have seen throughout his-
       tory. I refuse to accept their point of view. It has never
       been constructive. Every good man, if he was for prog-
       ress and social justice, has also defended the cause of
       women. I cannot believe that this progressivism, right
       on every other point, ran counter to nature, was anti-
       evolutionary, just on the question of women's rights and
       possibilities.

Vedo: It is a sorry fact, but true, that conservatives, pessimists, reactionaries, or whatever you call them, often have been more profound thinkers than the progressives. On the problem of womanhood, even the best among the progressives tend to be superficial. They slur over the facts of nature in a way that is amazing to behold.

Credo: Deep down I feel that here, too, there is something to what you say. Yet my reason refuses to accept it.

Vedo: If you are honest, you see what I see: that women are different from men; that, in physiological terms they are, in many respects, though not in all, inferior to men and have been so as far as our records reach back into the past; that this weakness, together with their more direct and prolonged concern with offspring, has determined their dependent position in the past, and nurture has only confirmed what nature proposed; that chivalry and charity have eased, are easing, the burden of their dependence on man; but that even full emancipation has not brought equality, because men and women are different, and not even millennia of equal opportunities will make them equal.

Credo: If everything you said just now were right, because it is what you see, what I see, the conclusion of your statement exceeds the bounds of your competence. What the future has in store is not for you to see. That is where pragma ends and dogma begins. I believe that even if women have been inferior in the past, they need not be so in the future; and I believe, therefore, in the *justice* of granting them equal rights and equal opportunities. If I am born a woman, an active woman, perhaps an ambitious woman—even though perhaps the mother of several children—I confess I need this faith, this conviction. For without it I could not go on working and striving. I should give up and querulously become one of the inferior beings you assert women to be. But faith, in our time, cannot be maintained without reasons. Therefore I must rationalize my conviction; I must reconcile what I honestly see with what I honestly believe. And therefore I am going to write this book: for my own justification, and for that of all liberal, progressive, and optimistic men and women alike, who hold that men and women are born with equal rights and equal possibilities.

ONE

The Birds and the Bees

The whole matter of sex may hark back to some of the basic aspects of mass physiology.

WARDER C. ALLEE[1]

The planets rolled around the stars, and the stars were fixed, and the movement was ordered and measured according to laws. But the laws revealed incongruities : the contrasting principles of relativity and of the constancy of the velocity of light. And if one was right, the other must be wrong. In considering the paradox, man's mind was governed by certain suppositions concerning time and space which appeared so self-evident and so absolute that no one ever doubted their truth.

But the stars turned in galaxies, and the galaxies moved through the universe, and the universe kept expanding. The adaptation of our notions concerning space and time to these dizzy dimensions produced formulae which are, in general, almost identical with those resulting from the old theories, for the latter were found to be in accord with experience. Still—or again—valid, they are reinterpreted, redimensioned, so to speak, in the context of the wider vision, and the incongruities are gone.

Human societies rose and fell and succeeded one another, and their movements were ordered and measured according to laws validated by experience and honored by time. But the laws revealed incongruities, contrasting principles : the unquestionable justice of granting equal rights to all individuals whether male or female, and the equally unquestionable inferiority of women throughout human history. And if one was right, the other must be wrong. In considering the paradox, men's minds were governed by certain suppositions concerning maleness, femaleness, inferiority, and superiority, which appeared to them so self-evident and so absolute that no one ever doubted their truth.

9

But human society is only a fleeting incident in the aeon-movement of evolution from protozoan matter to emerging spirit. The adaptation of our notions concerning male and female to these dizzy dimensions will produce formulae which will be, in general, almost identical with those resulting from the old, anthropocentric theory—as they must, for here again, as with our notions of time and space, the old formulae are found to be in accord with experience. They can be reinterpreted, re-dimensioned in the context of the wider vision, and the incongruities will be gone.

Maleness and femaleness in the animal kingdom! The variety of their expressions, and of their combinations, is endless.

The first living being that ever emerged out of the mud was rather female in character. "Rather," because femaleness makes no sense where there is no maleness. But the first living being did, more or less, what females kept doing later: it grew, matured, split up, grew, and matured again, deathless and aimless.

Protozoa coalesced into Metazoa; but even where individuality was more clearly delimited and organization more specialized, females, winged ones and in the watery main, went on busily laying unfertilized eggs and procreating, parthenogenetically, myriads of generations that knew no male.

Other species specialized in maleness and femaleness. There are kinds where the male, tiny and underdeveloped, lives as a parasite within the flourishing body of the female; in no sphere of primitive life does the male cut a great figure. Concern with offspring does not seem to detract from the female's other interests and possibilities. On the contrary: the species most fascinating to us humans, the social insects—because of their urbanistic genius, the complexity of their social organization, their invention of agriculture, slavery, and war, the high development of their language—are all basically feminine. The female's field of action is rich and varied, whereas the male's function is purely biological. After he has done his job of fertilizing, he is driven off or killed.

Among fish, in general, the male is more absorbed by the service to the species than is the female. The female lays her eggs and wanders on, carefree. The male is the homemaker. It is he who builds the nest, takes care of the eggs, and keeps the young in the nest until they are able to manage for themselves. The three-spined sticklebacks and the Labyrinthici have been frequently studied as exemplifying this type of male-female relationship.

Among birds, everything is possible: mother and father, for instance, can be equal partners with equal duties and equal rights—the ideal democratic family. They look alike and behave alike. They build their nest together, take turns on the eggs, and fill their offsprings' gaping mouths. Sometimes, in late years, it even happens that a female turns male; but considering their way of life, they derive scarcely any advantage from this rather incidental transformation.

Besides the species more understandable to humans, where the male fights his kind and conquers his territory, where he sings and shines in splendid colors, while the female, drab and silent, breeds and nurses—besides such species, there are other, queerer ones, where the female is larger and more conspicuous than the nest-bound, brooding male in his simple garb of protective coloring. There are species, such as certain quail, where the females fight each other with claws and beaks in bloody battles for the possession of their meek mates. These latter sit and brood, and if one of them be neglectful of nest and eggs or young, the imperious spouse will drive him home and rough him up so that his cinderella feathers fly. The females are polyandrous; they visit several males and lay their eggs in the nests of these.

Dominance and leadership are not the prerogatives of the male sex—not even among mammals. Dominance and aggressiveness shift back and forth according to the species and according to individuals. In some species, one sex is dominant during one season, the other during the next. Among red deer, Barbary sheep, domestic sheep, and goats, leadership plays an important social role and usually rests with the female. Biologists have stressed the value of this kind of "matriarchy" and have pointed out that it makes for true gregariousness and co-operation. The "social instinct" of the female is "selfless," unlike that of the male, who, where he is a leader in the animal kingdom, is a bully and a tyrant. Female-led herds, such as red deer, thus are larger than male-led herds, and better integrated in case of danger, when male-led herds tend to disintegrate. Though ornate and mighty, the male tends toward uselessness in his asociality, like the drone in a hive.

Where is the law in this jungle of patterns?

The only truth that can be abstracted thus far is a negative one: it is not true that maleness and femaleness are associated with absolute standards of behavior and value. It is not true that the female, because of her femaleness, is limited to care of offspring, nor that such care inhibits her other activities and abilities.

It is not true, furthermore, that maleness and femaleness are the two poles necessary for the creation of the current of life. Life went on before sexual differentiation, and would go on, presumably, even if this were to come to an end. The very origin of sex, incidentally, shows that it does not reflect a metaphysical duality, but is functional, determined by adventitious external factors.

Simple casual propinquity, as directed by wind and currents, proved advantageous to the primordial sexless beings. It facilitated existence in various ways: it increased resistance against poisons, waste products, or the danger of drying out. But more than that: it spurred the appetites, accelerated metabolism, and sped the process of reproduction. A single protozoan reproduced at a slower rate than did a member of a group. The group provided social or mutual incitement, a stimulating neighborliness which eventually became fusion.[2] The stronger partner absorbed the weaker. The stronger now became the female, which grew, and matured, and split. The weaker became the male.

Femaleness was the crown of success in life, at that stage: bulk, health, and maturity. Maleness was the measure of immaturity, misfortune, starvation, or injury. It was characterized by the absence of various organs. According to luck, or the lack thereof, one status or the other was attained—and not once and for all, but reversibly.

The annelid worm, for example, spends its youth and adolescence in maleness; at the zenith of maturity it switches to femaleness. The female phase may be continued until death, or, owing to some misfortune, the male phase may have to be resumed. When a few of the anterior segments of a functioning female are cut off, a tail regenerates on one piece, a head on the other; but, under this strain and stress, both regenerated worms are males. If conditions are favorable, each matures again into femaleness. When two females of this species meet, the more enterprising female may get herself a husband—or rather, two —by biting the other in half![3]

A marine-snail egg has been fertilized and is sinking to the bottom of the sea. Shall I be male? shall I be female? it is thinking on its way down. *Che serà, serà.* If there is no one down there, what a bore! No distraction, and the egg will grow heavy with solitude, and femaleness will be its reward. But there may be company. There may be, for instance, a male. Perhaps a small, uncomely one who won't be able to distract the new arrival from growing and maturing to femaleness. But he may be large and imposing, of almost female importance, and this will stunt the newcomer's growth. If, finally, the company is actually female, this will create a situation in which the newcomer will be distracted from growing; thus it will be doomed to maleness.

Inasmuch as this marine-snail reasoning is beyond the comprehension of our scientists, they must content themselves, as they do, with the observation that the mechanism of this influence is as yet unexplained. The fact remains, however, that for aeons of forgotten time, sex was determined not by internal but by external balance—by the relations with the outside world, by company, by group-*Gestalt*.

Number, the most elementary factor of social organization, should, of course, be expected to act on this balance. In fact, crowding does produce a change in the sex ratio.[4] And since femaleness, at this stage of evolution, implies a higher degree of development and individuation, it is logical that the effect of crowding should be masculinizing. Among water fleas, for example, it has been observed that males are produced by overcrowding. Whether this is due to the resulting shortage of food, to an accumulation of waste products, or to other, still obscure, causes, is not known at present. Certain nematode worms offer the same spectacle. These tiny worms are parasitic in insects. If only a few eggs are introduced into a grasshopper host, most of the hatching wormlets are female; but if many eggs are fed, the nematodes that hatch are almost all males. Why? The scientists say, we simply don't know.

Sex, we might say at the risk of shocking everybody, was an acquired character which in due time became hereditary. That is, first the sexual functionality of an individual was triggered off by external factors. Then the genetic mechanism infiltrated and took over. On a reduced time scale, this same process can be observed in the history of some species of social insects. Among the more primitive bees (*Bombidae*), sex is determined trophogenically, that is, by special diet administered in special cells of the hive; whereas among the more evolved species of *Meliponinae,* evidence has been given of the genetic distinction of queens and workers.[5]

The transfer of the mechanism triggering off the development of the sexual function from outside to inside, is, of course, only one aspect of the victory of inside over outside; that is, the increasing self-assertion of the individual over and against the environment, which includes the group. The emergence of the individual involves greater variability, and variability becomes an attribute of the male. The female, like the group, is biologically conservative.

But the action of the environment and, in particular, of the group, on the sexual constitution of the individual does not cease at the point at which sex determination becomes, apparently, internalized. Crowding still produces, and/or is produced by, a change in the sex ratio. But since maleness, now, implies a higher degree of individuation, it is logical that the effect of crowding should be feminizing, and/or, that the effect of feminizing should be crowding. This, in fact, can be observed on the most diverse levels of vertebrate life.

"Outbreaks" of rodents and ungulates, for instance, are due to a number of concomitant causes, some of them as yet quite obscure—a sudden formidable increase in fertility, for instance: more pregnant females; more females capable of pregnancy; a greater number of females. No systematic study of the change of the sex ratio in connection with such outbreaks is available, but such changes have been observed time and again, and enough figures, spread over numbers of works, could be cited to prove the point.

"Lemming years" coincide with the breeding of an excess of

females. Females and more females and more females. The colony grows from five thousand members to seventy-five thousand in one season and, with so many more females, to a million and a half in the next, and from there to forty-six million members and more. The food supply is exhausted. The spaces between animal and animal shrink; individual scurrying merges into the rippling on the surface of a new whole. The group-force increases. The individuals are transformed. They change their ways, they change their being. They grow hysterical and pugnacious, trampling down whatever comes their way, and heedlessly falling prey to the attacks of rapacious beasts and vindictive men. The home ground brims over with a heavy, bubbling soup of beasts, and they flow down over slopes and rocks, filling up holes, falling into cellars and basements. They push through lakes and rivers, incurring death without fear, the instinct of self-preservation—individuation's shield—having been thrown away and forgotten. Individuals die, as drops of water dry, but the torrent moves on and, in spite of all losses, grows into a stream. The migrating mass keeps growing, producing ever more fertile females, absorbing tributaries rushing down from neighboring mountains. The flowing together is due, the scientists say, to emotional disturbances which lead to an enfeeblement of individuality and a demand for support in cohesion with others. And the stream, as streams do, finally flows in horrid cascades into the sea. None of the lemmings ever returns. And the largest part of them were females.[6]

The springbok of Great Bushmanland, graceful, timid gazelles, go on similar death stampedes. Once every twenty years or so a marked excess of females may be produced. As with the lemmings, a mad multiplication sets in. The group-force grows, the individual is enfeebled, transformed. There follows an "emigration," westward ho, to the sea, from whence none returns. So prodigious is the death toll at the end of that great migration that one observer reported, "the desolate stretch of sandy shore reached by the flying horde was afterward piled, at high water mark, for a distance of thirty miles, with a continuous bank formed of the swollen dead bodies of vast numbers of the drowned emigrants, washed back to land by the waves." And, among the corpses, there was a marked excess of females.[7]

Other cases could be added, where the sudden increase in numbers, unleashing a group-force which translates itself into various forms of hysteria and enfeeblement of the individual, coincides with a change in the sex ratio in favor of the female; and many are the naturalists who have observed, and been puzzled by, this coincidence. Among mice, as among moths, a marked preponderance of females has been found to be associated with periods of phenomenal increase, but just why this happens, no one can explain.

Homo sapiens makes no exception to the rule. Crowding creates an excess of women, as can be ascertained by the student of the sex ratio in any large urban conglomeration as compared to that obtained in the sparsely settled countryside. And an excess of women means an increase of population, which may be checked, but not annulled, by the fact that we are dealing, by and large, with a monogamous species.

The contrary, also, is true. Shrinking populations shrivel up into melancholy groups of men. Of this, Huxley and the Wellses give the following account:

There should be mentioned the extremely high male sex ratio, up to 160 males per 100 females, found in some primitive peoples who are decreasing in numbers as a result of contact with civilization, e.g., the Melanesians and some North American Indians. This condition of affairs does not seem to be due to female infanticide, and for the present remains wholly unexplained. Whatever its causes, the paucity of women naturally helps the disappearance of the tribe.[8]

The same excess of males, perhaps due to inbreeding but, on the whole, unexplained and at any rate connected with the dwindling of group-force, has been observed by other naturalists in dying animal communities.

So much for the most primitive form of group-force, resulting from crowding, in the most primitive form of social organization: masculinizing at the bottom, feminizing higher up on the ladder of evolution.

The herd, the flock, the school, represent the next stage of social organization. Outbreaks are leaderless and inarticulate as is the dance of swarming moths. Group-force is engendered by sheer propinquity.

But in the herd, the flock, the school, this propinquity is willed, not random. The group-force begins to articulate and specialize. Less impetuous and elementary, its action is channeled over longer stretches of time and its effects on the relative position of the sexes is more complete.

Also at this stage the group-force engenders numerical superiority of the female: among deer and hollow-horned ruminants, as among fur seal and gregarious birds and fish. A number of explanations have been offered, and discarded. Since most of these species are polygamous, it has been claimed that the males kill one another while fighting for a harem. The females, however, outnumber the males even in species in which male combat with fatal results is unknown. For instance, among the ruff (*Philomachus pugnax,* pugnacious friend of battle), combat between the frilled and showy males is part of the courtship antics, not aimed at real killing. Yet the females outnumber the males. Stallions in love rear up and fall on one another and fight furiously, but no one has ever seen them kill one another. Yet there are more mares, many more, just as there are more females in any other herd of ungulates.

The distortion of the sex ratio in antlered game might be due to a greater mortality rate in the male sex that could be ascribed, partially at least, to exhaustion after the rut, spring starvation after the antlers are cast, or the greed of trophy hunters; but the distortion extends to areas far wider than the hunting grounds of antler-happy humans.

Whatever partial explanation may be adduced, whatever other factors may be at work on that complicated job of distorting the sex ratio, it is likely, at any rate, that the numerical preponderance of the female in herds, flocks, or schools, may "hark back to some of the basic aspects of mass physiology."[9]

But the action of the group-*Gestalt* on the sex balance of the group does not end here.

The group has a way of compensating for the numerical superiority of the female by making the male bulkier, mightier, and more formidable. And the greater the discrepancy in numbers, the more marked is the difference between male and female, the more polygamous is the species, and the more exclusively are sexual aggressiveness and display attributes of the male. Where the number of males roughly equals the number of females, sexual dimorphism is reduced to a minimum: the sexes look and act alike and, associated in monogamous families, they share the household chores and the obtaining of food. Finally, in those rare species where the males outnumber the females (exceptional on the higher rungs of the evolutionary scale), the female is larger than the male, and more colorful. Such a species is polyandrous, and display and aggressiveness are the prerogatives of the female. In *Homo sapiens* the females slightly outnumber the males, the males are slightly larger and some more formidable, display shifts from one to the other, and aggressiveness is common among both. It is a strangely logical world.

This is not all, but it is part of the whole, and it helps to see males and females, not as separate beings with absolute attributes, but as determined by a sexual balance, as a function of group-*Gestalt*. If the one changes, the other changes, too. And the function, in its turn, determines the structure—as always happens in biology. Display movements, for instance, engender conspicuous structures; prolonged inhibition in the lower ranks of the social hierarchy, on the other hand, stunts physical growth, as it hampers psychological development.

Just as the mechanism determining sexual functioning switched, at a certain moment, from external to internal, so with sex structure: the secondary sex characters are first and foremost determined from outside, by the group; then they become hereditary within each sex. But the group-force continues to act on them. Caste—with the sweeping changes in body structure it effects through the mutual influence of individuals upon one another—and sex, in this respect, show a similar development.

A striking example of group-force action on the secondary sex characters of the individual is provided by the locusts of South Africa. During their "solitary phase," these show strong sexual dimorphism; that is, the females are considerably larger than the males, and their colors are different. Then the swarming phase sets in, together with a state of excitement brought on partly as a reaction to physical stimuli such as body temperature and the sight of other insects, partly by more obscure factors of a psychological nature: the action of some sort of "social gene," tentatively called "locustine." Under its influence males and females undergo a transformation, approaching one another in size and coloring, so that, when the swarming phase is in full swing, both sexes look and act alike.[10] This brings to mind Freud's observation of the antagonism between group-force and "directly sexual tendency": where the former wins out, "the distinction between the sexes plays no part."[11]

If random conglomeration, plagues, and outbreaks engender a first-degree group-force which translates itself into numerical superiority of one sex or the other; if herds, flocks, and schools exemplify an intermediate stage of association, engendering a second-degree group-force which acts on the sex ratio as well as on the psychological and physical structures of its members; then the last and highest degree of group-force is released by the organizations of social insects. The literature in this field is so vast and has become, from Maeterlinck's[12] and von Frisch's[13] bees to Schneirla's[14] and Wheeler's[15] ants, so popular that it would be useless to attempt a drawn-out secondhand description of the phenomenon. It may suffice to remember that the more advanced phylogenetically the social evolution of a species, the more marked is the pre-eminence of the female and the subordination of the only intermittently functioning male. The most highly socialized species—honey bees and ants—which constitute the most perfect pattern of "collectivism," with the group and its numbers determining the physiology and psychology of the members, are, in the words of Wheeler, "frankly female, the male being reduced to a merely temporary fecundative agency," while the female not only does the nursing of the young, but the foraging and the constructing, the soldiering and the organizing. Wheeler observes, in a footnote, the similarity of the psychological make-up of these "frankly female" societies and that of a human mob: "high emotivity, suggestibility, rage, etc. . . . These manifestations, moreover, occur only in populous colonies, since a mob implies a number of co-operating individuals; feeble or incipient colonies of bees, wasps, and ants are always very timid."[16]

The termites are the only species in the world where the male, too, has been socialized and where, with an approximately even sex ratio, the offices of soldier and worker are evenly distributed among males and females. But even in this society Wheeler

notes a "female pre-eminence . . . as shown by the enormous
somatic and gonadic development of the queens in the higher
species."

Thus, the group-force acts on the sex balance of the whole,
and on the function and structure of each of its members,
throughout the animal kingdom, from Protozoa to *Homo
sapiens*. But while it tends to "masculinize" at the most primitive levels of life, this trend is reversed at the approximate moment when the individual asserts itself over and against its
environment to the point of making sex "inner-determined" and
inherent in the inheritable mass. The rise of the individual and
the rise of the male, from then on, are parallel developments.
Progressive individualism equals emerging maleness. Insofar as
evolution proceeds through selection based on struggle, it proceeds, on the whole, through the male. Born of adversity, the
male thrives on adversity, evolution's romantic child.

But the "struggle for life" is of limited value, an agent of
short-range progress. If this were the only factor, all of us
would still be a loose bunch of Protozoa, after aeons of struggle.

The "struggle for life" makes sense only against the background of co-operation—the long-range agent of evolution—
which rises from sheer physiological proximity, orders and
specializes and binds, fills the interstices, until, out of casual
conglomeration, a new organism arises: a new individual. And,
insofar as evolution proceeds through co-operation, it proceeds
through the female. Group-maker from the beginning, the
female thrives on the forces which the group in turn releases:
evolution's archaic-futuristic child. "This phase of the social
implications of sex has escaped general comment," observed
Warder Allee, a pioneer in the field of animal ecology whose
findings have not yet been fully exploited by sociologists studying the human species. "I first heard it mentioned by the late

Professor Wheeler. Apparently when there is a social difference between the sexes, it is the females that are the more and the males the less social; and the few striking exceptions only confirm the rule."[17]

But if all were left to this kind of co-operation, we should be a colony of corals, a hive of soldiering ants, stabilized in aeons of organization.

Where co-operation and selection are duly dosed, where organization and random variation, female conservatism and male innovation are duly balanced, there the rate of progress is greatest in the animal kingdom.

Where does all this leave us with regard to *Homo sapiens*?

The role of the individual has increased in importance throughout evolution, and man, at least the temporary peak of evolution, has reached, with his brain capacity, his infinite adaptability, a high point of individuation. Looking at our species from this angle and in this context, one should not be surprised to find it male-dominated, to see the female inferior. And if women are smaller and weaker, if their blood is "thinner," their brain weight inferior, their reactions slower, their creativeness inhibited by hormonic functions, this is due, also, to environment. Not in the sense proposed by John Stuart Mill however, that is, to be ascribed to some primal and unexplained conquest by man who has held her in "subjection" ever since. The inferiority of women is a result of the species' position on the evolutionary scale: man the triumpher over his environment; man the measure; man the mind; man the universe.[18]

But this position is not unequivocal. For while representing the peak of individuation, mankind has achieved also the maximum of socialization—surpassed, in the animal kingdom, only by the social insects. But whereas socialization among the insects is biological, organic, and thus involves absolute female supremacy, in the human species socialization is cultural, that is, secondary; and though socialization acts on the mental and physical structure of the individual—the sex ratio! the "feminization" of modern man!—this action remains balanced by man's organic tendency toward a less gregarious life and greater individuation.

Every species has its place defined somewhere between the poles of solitariness and socialization, and its sex balance is determined accordingly. *Homo sapiens* alone is conscious of the tension between the two. Thus woman does not know her place.

In *Homo sapiens,* furthermore, and only here, has natural evolution been superseded by cultural evolution, which—as biologists, anthropologists and natural philosophers alike have pointed out—while following the laws of natural evolution, has accelerated its tempo, so that it constitutes, at one and the same time, its continuation and its recapitulation. *Recapitulation,* insofar as it reflects, on a minute scale, the great movements of natural evolution: the evolution of the individual and the evolution of social behavior, with women's position and women's nature suspended between the two—gaining in collectivist moments of history, losing with individualism. *Continuation,* inasmuch as it will carry the species further, beyond the foreseeable.

Where to?

Evolution is determined by the group's current vision of destiny. If certain trends—already obsolete—had prevailed, asserting the absolute importance of the group over and against the total insignificance of the individual, masculine men might have degenerated, and their number shrunk. The reproductive function might have been taken over by the State, specialized, and rendered largely artificial, thus freeing women, psychologically and physiologically, for every kind of hive duty. They wouldn't have been nice women, probably; they would have lacked all womanly charm. Some supertype of a *Bund Deutscher Mädel;* some caricature of a Communist woman functionary.

Deviationists of every description having been eliminated, the fate of the species would have been stabilized like that of the ants. But deviationists would have kept cropping up, forming, perhaps, a new species; for the evolution of the individual is a tendency too well-established by natural evolution throughout the realm of life to be reversed by cultural evolution.

Rugged individualism, on the other hand, would have been no less anti-evolutionary than this kind of socialization. Living in small, autarchic groups, consisting of one male with one or more adult females and their immature offspring, man, stocky and with a lot of hair on his chest, would have kept bossing his small, sleek, and dependent mate; but highly individualized, that is, variable, as he would have been, he couldn't have helped, in the long run, inventing everything all over again, including the evolution of social behavior, without which all individual inventions come to naught. This, however, would have carried the women to the foreground.

The long-range function of cultural evolution would seem to be that of integrating the two trends of natural evolution: individuation and socialization. That this integration is under way now, or, at least, ought to be or wants to be, we, who live in the twentieth century, are, indeed, painfully aware. And, harking back to some of the basic aspects of mass physiology, it is bound to affect the sex balance of the species, to change relations between men and women, to act on their psychological and physical evolution, making them equal. That this transformation is under way now, or ought to be or wants to be, of this, also, we are aware.

To sum up, we see that woman has been man's inferior because of our species' position on the scale of natural evolution toward individuation, and the sex balance resulting from this "environment." Throughout the animal kingdom, sex-linked inferiority is relative, conditioned, and reversible.

We believe that a new, specifically human, cultural synthesis of the natural trends of individuation and socialization will change the sex balance and produce superior women, men's true equals. Therefore, laws and customs advancing women's freedom and equality are not anti-historical, not anti-biological, not anti-logical, not concessions of chivalry or tolerance; they anticipate, as all good laws should, a state toward which mankind is moving, while, at the same time, helping it to move there. We believe, therefore, that they are in harmony, in full accord, with evolution, which is the touchstone of ethics.

Women and Crowds
The Group-Force Space-Vector

Women's emergence has come at the same time as our marked collectivity, our drift toward crowd values, our belief in an equality so loosely and widely held that it resembles a passionate longing more than a belief, that everyone and everything shall be as alike as possible.

FLORIDA SCOTT-MAXWELL[1]

The crowd engenders a force, a group-force, which has no moral, cognitive, or emotional qualities. It is a physical force. This group-force has, in fact, been compared to the field-force in physics, the group or crowd taking the place of a gravitational or electromagnetic field, and the individual corresponding to the atom. Just as the field-force acts on the atoms, or atomic particles, transforming them, creating new relations among them, so the group-force acts on the individuals, transforming them, creating new relations among them,[2] new fields—energy out of matter—around each of them.

The nature of this group-force or social field-force has only recently become an object of scientific studies. And the more it is studied, the more elementary it appears, both in its origin and in its action, moving on a plane where the psychological and the physiological meet and interact.

Group-force is engendered by sheer physical proximity, by density, by numbers. Number is a quantitative factor. But it acts on the character and the nature—which are qualitative factors— of the components of the group, bringing out hidden, subconscious traits, or superimposing new traits which, in the isolated individual, did not hitherto exist.

A French sociologist, Alfred Sauvy, has recently called attention to the relationship between quantity and quality—or at least one aspect of it: the dominance relationship between the members of a group. "Between the numbers of men (or their 'pressure') and the domination which is exercised upon them, various relationships exist. . . . These relationships are often so

29

markedly reciprocal that, as against the difficulty of separating cause from effect, it seems preferable to speak simply of accommodation or even of relative harmony."[3]

Another sociologist, John Boodin, points out analogously, that "density of population is a factor in social organization. . . . It has been shown by sociologists that the density or sparseness of a population makes a great deal of difference with regard to the activities and problems that arise. . . . Social integration must be considered as through-and-through relationship, an interpenetration within common purposes, where the individual components are modified by the common bond, past and present."[4]

This theory is so well-established now that we need not document it further. David Riesman's thesis of the influence of the "potential growth rate" of a population—a quantitative factor —on the character of its components ("tradition-directed," "inner-directed," "other-directed"*), fits into this context.[5] As in the electromagnetic field, the action is reciprocal.

Density is a basic group-force engendering factor. But unlike the case in physics, where the field-force has only a space dimension, the group-force has also a time dimension. Where it acts in time, time-density—tradition—takes the place of space-density —numbers. Time-vector and space-vector at times act concurrently; at other times they pull in different directions. The nature of the changes wrought on the individual depends on the resultant of the two.

That the group-force time-vector engenders a considerable amount of femininity has been amply demonstrated by Bachofen, Jung, and others: witness the feminine, matriarchal ele-

---

* The coincidence in time is not always complete. For example, China today is still in a phase of "transitional growth," which should make the population "inner-directed." But the Chinese already are strongly "other-directed." The same holds true today of the world population as a whole. The phase of "inner-directedness" has been foreshortened, more condensed, than that of "transitional growth." In spite of this derangement in time, Riesman's theory remains a most useful working hypothesis.

ments of myth and lore, projections all of man's collective subconscious, the *anima*, which, according to Jung, *is* feminine. We shall come back to this in Chapter III.

The group-force space-vector affects the individual in various ways. It alters the relations between men and women. It emphasizes traits which tradition and science alike have associated with the "feminine."

Freud notes that in the "primal horde"—that is, the collective whose group-force is at a maximum (and whose psychology survives or recurs in any crowd formation even today)—common activity is all-pervasive. It excludes nothing, not even the excremental function. The one great exception is provided by the sexual act. The love relations between men and women remain outside the group. Therefore, "Even where groups are formed which are composed of both men and women, the distinction between the sexes plays no part." For, "if directly sexual tendencies become too strong, they disintegrate every group formation." Since "directly sexual tendencies" are antisocial, the group-force acting on collectivistic societies tends to play them down, to diminish their importance.[6]

Freud derived his theory from his observations of minor "artificial organizations" such as churches and armies. He wrote too early to see his theory verified on a large scale in the great collectivistic or other-directed states of our day. He would have found it confirmed in Russia and in China, and also in the United States. All three states are strongly collectivistic, with the group-force engendering a high degree of other-directedness, no matter whether on a capitalistic or on a communistic economic basis. The puritanism of the Russians and Chinese, as manifested in their movies, their literature, their mores, and the public overconcern with sex manifested in the American entertainment and publicity industries, are, fundamentally, equally anti-sexual. Men and women in other-directed societies tend to be alike and to perform the same functions. This is due to the action of the group-force.*

Where the group-force, reaching its maximum, engenders collective frenzy and mass hysteria, its de-sexualizing tendency is driven to the logical ultimate: witness the ageless and recurrent scenes of self-castration of fanatical crowds. The mass following of Ishtar or Ashtarte in the ancient Middle East was regularly seized by fits of collective delirium, and hundreds and thousands of men laid hands on themselves and in one wild orgy sacrificed all their virility to the goddess. The women, who constituted a large part of the goddess' mass retinue, likewise were gripped by the frenzy, cut off their own breasts and performed other self-mutilations. The history of the ancient Celts, and the Dahomey Amazons and others, records similar events. In a book on collective frenzies, *Foules en Delire,* de Félice recalls examples of mass self-castration as late as the nineteenth century among the sect of dancers and jumpers in Russia *(chlustes)*. Between 1840 and 1859, official statistics (registering only those cases that had been recorded by the police) counted 1550 men who committed self-castration, and 825 women showing various forms of grave self-mutilation, such as ablation of the breasts.[7]

The group-force, then, tends to minimize sexual differences and to equalize men and women. But there are other ways in which it acts on the sex balance and, in a way, makes the "crowd"—and the "other-directed" society—"behave like women."

"Crowds behave like women" has indeed been said for thousand of years: the Greeks said so; the Romans said so; Gustave

* That the same was true under Nazism and Fascism is shown in Chapter VIII.

Le Bon said so; Hitler said so. "Women behave like crowds" would seem to be a more startling statement. Both statements imply that there must be a set of attributes common to the behavior of crowds and women.

In general, these attributes are not flattering. And the analogy, on the whole, has been drawn by men who were upset by both women and crowds.

Le Bon[8], Ortega y Gasset[9], Reiwald[10] : these still are the great testimonies of "mass psychology," revalidated, more recently, by David Riesman, whose "other-directed" man shares many traits with Ortega's "mass man."

This "mass psychology" is not to be confused with the more positive theories of "group dynamics," a more recent science : the science of the era of the Ascent of Woman. But let us have a look at the older, traditional statements on crowds and women.

Women, like crowds, they say, are super-emotional.

Women, like crowds, are egocentric.

Women, like crowds, are unstable on the surface, below which, in women as in crowds, flows a broad stream of conservatism.

According to Le Bon, the crowd is "impulsive" and "irritable ... unable to think logically ... lacking judgment and critique." The crowd exults in an "exaggeration of sentiment."[11]

All these are epithets familiarly applied to woman. "Be quite the woman, sway'd by each desire that bridleless impels you to and fro," Goethe's Thoas exhorts Iphigenia; and Diderot observes : "It is especially in the passions of love, the attacks of jealousy, the instincts of superstition, the way in which they share epidemic emotion, that women astonish us. . . . A woman carries within her an organ capable of terrible spasms which do as they will with her and excite in her phantoms of all kinds."[12]

"Since the stimuli that act on crowds are ever changing," says

Le Bon, "and since the masses obey them constantly, it follows
that the masses are utterly changeable." And Goethe says:

*"Vorschnell und töricht, echt wahrhaftes Weibsgebild,
Vom Augenblick abhängig, Spiel der Witterung, des
Glücks and Unglücks ..."*[13]

("Impetuous and foolish, perfect woman-type. Dependent
on the moment, sport of every breeze, of good and evil
fortune ...")

The notion that women are changeable has been transmitted
from people to people, from age to age. *Genus mutabile,* Vergil
calls womanhood; the French say, *"Souvent femme varie";* and
in *La donna è mobile* the idea found its music and conquered the
world.

"Never," says Le Bon concerning crowds, "did they direct
their sympathies toward benevolent masters, but toward tyrants,
to be ruled by them forcefully." And Hitler said, "Like women
they prefer to be mastered by strong men to mastering weak
men."[14]

The masculine type that arouses enthusiasm in the masses
seldom fails to impress women—who, of course, are part of
the masses. In Otto Weininger's terms, one might say that the
sexual complement of women and of the crowd is the same.

"The feelings of the crowd," says Le Bon, "are exaggerated
and simple. This one-sidedness and exuberance of feeling pro-
tects crowds against doubt and uncertainty. Like women, they
immediately go to extremes."

Women show extremes in virtue or extremes in vice. The
good woman, it has been said, is better than the good man. Even
Nietzsche, no feminist, was of this opinion: "The perfect woman
represents a higher type of human being than the perfect man.
Zoology offers the means to prove this statement."[15] And the
bad woman is worse than the bad man. Like the crimes of the

mob, "the crimes of women are usually more marked by cruelty than those of men," Havelock Ellis noted;[16] and this observation has been confirmed by Lombroso[17] and later penalists and psychologists.

Woman, like crowds, it is said, can be either completely good or completely bad, whereas man's character more usually is composed of good and evil. Or: women, like crowds, tend to be one-dimensional whereas man is multidimensional. Or: woman's virtue is monolithic whereas man's virtues are many and graded.

Euripides' women say, in *Iphigenia at Aulis:*

> *Glorious the quest of virtue is for us,*
> *the cloistered virtue, chastity.*
> *But for the man—his inborn grace*
> *of law and order maketh great,*
> *by service of her sons, the state:*
> *His virtue works a thousand ways.*

Yeats explains this "monolithic" character of woman:

Women, because the main event of their lives has been a giving themselves and giving birth, give all to an opinion as if it were some terrible stone doll. Men take up an opinion lightly and are easily false to it, and when faithful, keep the habit of many interests. We still see the world, if we are of strong mind and body, with considerate eyes, but to women, opinions become as their children or their sweethearts, and the greater their emotional capacity, the more do they forget all other things. They grow cruel, as if in defense of lover or child, and all this is done "for something other than human life." At last the opinion is so much identified with their natures that it seems a part of their flesh, becomes stone and passes out of life.[18]

This takes us to another, profounder trait that has been observed in women, as in crowds. Le Bon says:

The history of the people's revolutions can hardly be understood if one does not take into account the force of inertia acting within the crowds. They desire to change the names of their institutions; but the essence of these institutions is far too much the expression of the hereditary needs of the race, not to return always anew. The ceaseless changeability of the crowds extends only to the surface of things. In truth, they are ruled by an instinct of inertia . . . and by a fetishist veneration of tradition, an unconscious horror of everything new.

Wondering "how ideas settle down in the soul of the crowd," Le Bon observed, "how toilsome it is for them to penetrate the crowd, and what power they then gain over them."

In the more benevolent words of Cicero: "The people, though they are not so prone to find out truth by themselves as to follow custom or run into error, yet, if they be shown truth, they not only acknowledge and embrace it very suddenly, but are most constant and faithful guardians of it."[19]

Martin Luther noticed this same force of inertia acting in women. At first they are reluctant, "but once they accept the teaching of the evangelium, they are much stronger and far more ardent in believing, hold it much more stiffly and tenaciously than men."[20]

Biologically, woman's "inertia" coincides with what Havelock Ellis called "woman's organic tendency, notwithstanding all their facility for minor oscillations, to stability and conservatism."[21] The smaller size of women is a consequence of this conservatism. "There can be little doubt that the smaller size of women as compared to men is connected with the preservation of a primitive character. Zoologists believe that the early or ancestral members of a group are of small size, and that the study of smaller members within given groups of animals promises the best results as to their phylogeny. Women by their smaller size approximate the probably smaller stature of man's ancestors."

Sociologically, this force of inertia, acting below a veneer of

changeability, has made of woman "the stable element," passing
on, from generation to generation, along with the mother
tongue, the same crafts, the same knowledge, and the same
superstitions. *Facilius enim mulieres incorruptam antiquitatem
conservant*,[22] says Cicero ("Women more easily preserve antiquity intact"). And Aristophanes jests:

> *First they dye their wools*
> *with boiling tinctures, in the ancient style.*
> *You won't find them, I warrant, in a hurry*
> *trying new plans. . . .*
> *They roast their barley, sitting, as of old;*
> *they on their heads bear burdens, as of old;*
> *they keep their Thesmophors, as of old;*
> *they bake their honied cheese cakes, as of old;*
> *they victimize their husbands, as of old;*
> *they still secrete their lovers, as of old;*
> *they buy themselves sly dainties, as of old;*
> *they like a woman's pleasures, as of old. . . .*[23]

Other quotations could be added ad infinitum. The fact is
that throughout Western history, woman's mind and the mind
of the crowds or masses have been described in identical terms,
and over and over again analogies have been drawn between
them.

The older school of psychoanalysis likewise projects an
image of woman that has crowd features. This image—Freud's,
Helene Deutsch's, and partly, even, Simone de Beauvoir's—is
characterized by three basic traits: passivity, masochism, and
narcissism.

Passivity, or at least, in Freud's terms, a "preference for pas-
sive aims,"[24] which even may "require a good deal of activity to
achieve," derives from the feminine role in the sexual act, but

determines the whole psychological make-up of woman. Masochism and narcissism seem to constitute a set of mutually complementary, in the normal case reciprocally balancing, factors,
based on this passivity.

Masochism has been derived from the inseparable connection
between pleasure and pain in the feminine reproductive function. According to Helene Deutsch,* woman, in one of her functions, "must have a certain amount of masochism if she is to be
adjusted to reality. This is the reproductive function: from beginning to end [menstruation, defloration, pregnancy, child-
birth] it requires toleration of considerable pain. . . . Thus,
feminine sexuality acquires a masochistic character. Actually a
certain amount of masochism as psychological preparation for
adjustment to the sexual function is necessary in women."[25]

Feminine narcissism has been explained as a defense mechanism to offset the self-destructive effects of feminine masochism.
"Since the sexual tendencies of women are directed toward goals
that are dangerous for the ego, the latter defends itself and
strengthens its inner security by intensifying its self-love which
then manifests itself in narcissism."[26]

Add to this that the lack of a masculine genital organ, according to Freud, arouses an everlasting "penis envy"; that the Oedi-
pus complex directing sexual desire toward the father is not
counteracted, as in the case of boys, by fear of a formidable
father image and, owing to this lack of conflict between love
and fear, no strong superego can be created; that, lastly, girls
have more trouble in adjusting from the infantile to the adult
phase of sexuality and this difficulty absorbs the energies which
in boys are sublimated in cultural activities—all this being the
explanation for women's inferior contribution to culture
throughout history—and the picture we get of woman is dreary

* "Strange pleasure women take to speak of sister women nothing good."
Euripides

indeed : an envious, frustrated, "alienated" creature. One even wonders how she could have done as well as she actually has.

According to Freud and the Freudians, her psychological structure is physiologically and anatomically determined, therefore universal and unchangeable, even though limited more or less by the simultaneous presence of masculine traits. "It is," Freud says, "as though the individual were neither man nor woman but both at the same time, only rather more the one than the other. . . ,"[27] a theory that was carried to its wild climax by Otto Weininger.[28]

Passivity, masochism, and narcissism indeed are not monopolies of the weaker sex. They are ingredients in the psychological make-up of any human, or subhuman, being. But we may tentatively accept the evidence offered by the psychiatrists that, in our culture at least, the relative weight of these qualities increases as we go from the masculine man to the feminine man, from the feminine man to the masculine woman, and, finally, to the truly feminine woman. But it also increases as our observation passes from the individual to the group. The more collectivist the group, the more powerful the action of the group-force on the individual mind, the more tangibly emerge these "feminine qualities."

This passivity-activity, or female-male, relationship between masses and leaders has been noted by Alfred Adler, Paul Reiwald, and innumerable others.

Alfred Adler sees in the psychology of the leader a "masculine revolt," the urge to become virile.[29] Paul Reiwald finds that "it can't be chance that so many 'leaders' keep insisting on the feminine character of the masses. This emphasis not only increases the pathos of distance between leader and masses; it also reinforces and justifies the leader's own tendency 'to be on top,' to be the man."[30]

Externally, the male-female relationship between leader and

masses is often reflected in the pomp, visual and vocal, with
which the leader surrounds himself in approaching the masses.
While this phenomenon is an essential characteristic of any collectivist situation—even where the "leader" is a group of "Hidden Persuaders"—it survives most tangibly in ritual or magical
collective scenes, for instance the processions of the Catholic
Church, or in primitive societies.

We pick, at random, Bowdich's description of his reception
by the King of the Ashanti in 1817: "The King appears before
his assembled people in the midst of a pageant of elephants, peli-
cans, music, fine odors, arms and swords of gold; in his suite we
find courtiers dressed in the most showy cloths and silks and
crowned with crescents. They bear canopies, umbrellas of wonderful colors, scarlet and yellow on the inside, which they open
and close with brilliant effects."[31]

No scene could demonstrate more dramatically the male-female relationship between the leader and the masses: the wooing,
with all the splendor of brilliant colors, seductive shapes, excit-
ing scents, alluring voices and impressive weapons. And we need
not go into the details of the ecstasy aroused by these means
within the masses—their yielding, the much cited "rape of the
masses," their readiness to undertake anything for the leader's
sake, etc.—to complete the picture of this relationship.

The narcissism of the masses is a phenomenon as evident as
its passivity. It expresses itself in nationalism, racism, and other
such attitudes which are stable attributes of the totalitarian (and
other-directed) mass State. The stronger the group-force action,
the more marked are these traits, which are incompatible with
the rationalism of individualist societies.

As in the feminine psyche, narcissism is stressed to offset
the effects of masochism. For collective masochism, too, is a
phenomenon to be taken into account. Group-force action is accelerated, as is well-known, by frustration and want and the

ensuing self-abandonment. Collectivism thrives on the self-destructiveness of the individual. It is dangerous to the ego.

Freud and the older Freudians, of course, were individualists. They did not give any weight to man's innate tendencies to cooperate, but stressed his "death instinct," his aggressiveness, which would disrupt any society unless it were held together by strong leadership. Thus, according to Freud, any society will consist of a small elite of leaders, and a large mass of those led. David Riesman has compared these conclusions with those reached by Thomas Hobbes, "the great theorist of autocracy," who said that without absolute power having been vested in a sovereign, all men would be in a continuous state of war "of every man against every man . . . no arts, no letters, no society, and, which is worst of all, continual fear, and danger of violent death; and the life of man, solitary, poor, nasty, brutish, and short."[32]

In most of his work, Freud was not concerned with social but with individual destiny. More recent psychologists and analysts —Karen Horney, Erich Fromm—moving from Alfred Adler's *Gemeinschaftsgefühl* and approaching the individual from the sociological angle, have demolished the image of women created by the earlier Freudians.

"The realization that in different societies women fulfill different social functions and accordingly display different attitudes and mental characteristics, has shattered the idea of the all-powerful influence of anatomy and biological facts on character traits," states Viola Klein in her excellent little book, *The Feminine Character*.[33] Others—Clara Thompson, for example —have succeeded in accounting for every single trait of Freud's biologically rooted character structure as a result of "cultural pressure."[34] That the individualist thinker's conception of woman is intrinsically hostile while the more "collectivist" oriented thinkers are far kindlier toward her is, of course, not to be attributed to simple chance. We shall come back to this in Chapters VI and VII.

But whether "the feminine character" be determined by cultural evolution or by natural evolution makes relatively little difference with regard to the question: is there an affinity between the character traits brought out by the group-force and the feminine character? For many of the traits observed by Freud during the limited period of his work within a limited culture are, as Viola Klein herself points out, at any rate valid, "with corresponding modifications, in every society with a strong patriarchal tradition."[35] That is, they are valid for women in historical times practically everywhere. And whether inherited or acquired, intrinsically feminine or imposed on woman by her position—"the dominated sex," the "outgroup," "the other," "alienated"—it is these traits that must be compared to those superimposed by, or reacting to, the group-force.

In his recent *Comparative Psychology,* F. A. Moss writes:

In human beings, it has appeared to be a universal fact that, other things being equal, there is a negligible difference between males and females in cognitive capacities. And the findings in sub-human species have been similar. . . . It seems very probable that if a behavior difference between the sexes exists, it will be in emotional domains. In human beings, measurements of neuroticism by the Thurstone personality inventory and those of annoyance by Cason indicate that in these domains a very evident difference between the sexes appears, and it is significant that also in the experiments by Hall on emotionality in rats, very evident sex differences appear. Greater activity has been noted in the females, the predominance being greatest at the peak of the sexual cycle.[36]

Emotionality, emotions, are group-forming; analytic reason, logic, is separating, appertains to the individual. In evolutionary terms, analytic reason is a more recent "mutation," and mutations, in general, make their appearance first in the male and, only after they are well-established there, are acquired by the female, until finally the young take them over. It is therefore plausible that reason, rationality, logic, also should first have been attributes of men, although women have long since begun to acquire these qualities and will undoubtedly acquire them eventually as fully as men. Just as the females of other species have acquired horns, beards, or colored plumage.

To say, on the one hand, that the emotional aspects of the human psyche are *older,* pre-individual and group-forming and, on the other, that they are more intact in women than in men, simply translates Jung's *anima* theory into evolutionary terms.

But in spite of the difference between masculine and feminine emotionality[37] it is not true that women, as individuals, are more suggestible than men. This is demonstrated by Aldous Huxley in *Brave New World Revisited.* Describing a recent experiment conducted at the Massachusetts General Hospital on the pain-relieving effects of placebos—"anything which the patient believes to be an active drug, but which in fact is pharmacologically inactive"—he concludes:

In this experiment the subjects were one hundred and sixty-two patients who had just come out of surgery and were all in considerable pain. Whenever a patient asked for medication, to relieve pain, he or she was given an injection, either of morphine or of the placebo. About thirty per cent of the patients never obtained relief from the placebo. On the other hand, fourteen per cent obtained relief after every injection of distilled water. The remaining fifty-five per cent of the patients were relieved by the placebo on some occasions but not on others. In what respect did the suggestible reactors differ from the unsuggestible nonreactors? Careful study and testing revealed that neither age nor sex was a significant factor. Men reacted to the placebo as frequently as did women.[38]

It would seem that in situations not involving a group-force, women, as individuals, are no more suggestible than men.

If, nevertheless, women, at all times and in the most different sets of circumstances, have more easily fallen prey to collective frenzy, or shared "epidemic emotions," this may be explained by the affinity of their minds and the crowds' mind. The group-force acts more directly on women than on men; or, on the average—and in dealing with a group-force we are by definition concerned only with the average—the group-force acts on a larger section of the mind in the case of women. This affinity, intuited over the millennia by philosophers and poets, becomes plausible, palpable, in evolutionary and psychoanalytic terms without implying any contempt or hostility for women or prejudice as to their future.

"We have, therefore, to recognize," writes Havelock Ellis, "that in men, as in males generally, there is an organic variational tendency to diverge from the average; in women, as in females generally, there is an organic tendency, notwithstanding all their facility for minor oscillations, to stability and conservatism, involving a *diminished individualism and variability.*"

The words we have italicized point to the core of the affinity between the feminine character and the group-force-induced character. For the group-force, undoubtedly, induces "a diminished individualism and variability."

There is, however, one phase in the life of women in which their individualism is particularly "diminished," or, more than that, blurred, and that is during pregnancy. The following observations are from the diary notes of a young mother:

Sickness, in general, reveals the character of a man or woman. You know a person more truly if you have known him during a grave sickness. A strong person will be stronger in this situation, a weak one weaker, a gentle one gentler, a bitter one, still more bitter. Pregnancy alone, of all physical conditions, alters the character. Traits are imposed on the pregnant woman that are alien to her.

My face in the mirror looked alien to me. My character blurred. Childish violent desires, unknown to me, came over me, and childish violent dislikes. I am a coldly logical thinker, but at that time, my reasoning blurred and dissolved, impotent, into tears, another helpless, childish creature's tears, not mine. I was one and the other at once. It stirred inside of me. Could I control its movements with my will? Sometimes I thought I could, at other times I realized it was beyond my control. I couldn't control anything. I was not myself. And not for a brief passing moment of rapture, which men, too, may experience, but for nine quiet watchful months. . . . Then it was born. I heard it scream with a voice that was no longer mine. I heard the obstetrician say: "There it is, a nice little girl." And then he sang a phrase from a German war song about the "good comrade," who was shot down and lay at his feet: *"als wärs ein Stück von mir, als wärs ein Stück von mir."* (as though he were a piece of myself). And that was just the way I felt. . . .

There is something awfully "middle" about the whole business of sexual dimorphism and its social and psychological corollaries and problems.

"Middle" in the life of the individual: children are just children, and old age tends to erase secondary sex characters.

"Middle" in the life of the species, which, in general, shows little sexual dimorphism during the early phase of evolution, and much during the mid-phase, until, in many cases, the two sexes again become indistinguishable.

"Middle" on the social scale: among the working class, as among kings and queens, there is no women's problem, no dominant sex—the women's problem is first and foremost a middle-class problem.

"Middle" on the scale of intellectual values: the mass man, as we have seen, tends to minimize sexual dimorphism; genius has either no sex, or some of both.

"Middle," in all probability, in the evolution of life as a whole, which may well be passing from a pre-sexual through a bisexual to a post-sexual phase, where science may perpetuate the genetic advantages of variability and selection, and spiritual love supersede carnal love.

In human history the three phases correspond closely to those described by Erich Kahler: ". . . history appears as an evolution leading from the pre-individual community, to the post-individual community, through the development and completion of the individual."[39]

A look at one exemplary post-individual mass society of our day, namely our own, in which woman's "emergence has come at the same time as our marked collectivity,"[40] reveals some amazing and amusing, if incidental, similarities to the matriarchal societies of prehistory, as recorded by Bachofen and others.

Our society is, to the highest degree, an industrial society; but long before modern industrialism had reached its present American peak of development, Havelock Ellis noted: "Modern civilization is becoming industrial, that is to say, feminine in character, for the industries belonged primitively to women, and they tend to make men like women. . . ."[41] The larger-headed, delicate-faced, small-boned man of urban industrial civilization is, in fact, much closer to the typical woman than is the savage.

In pre-individual society, likewise, matriarchism and industrialism went hand in hand. Industrialism devaluated masculine virtues and strengthened the position of women. Bachofen[42] quotes the example of the Boeotians, and the people of Egypt, where the men sat at the loom and the women roamed about in the market squares. Industry physically soiled and degraded men; as a consequence, women became freer and superior. That the consequences of this inversion of status went pretty far is indicated by Herodotus (II, 35): "Among them [the Egyptians] the women buy and sell, the men abide at home and weave . . . . Men carry burdens on their heads, women on their shoulders; women make water standing, men sitting. . . ."

With reference to ancient, matriarchal Egypt, Bachofen has this further observation:

It may not be superfluous to note to what extent the materialistic [in the literal sense of the word: matter-bound, *stofflich*] mother principle must further the quick assimilation of immigrant peoples to the native stock. The situation prevailing in Egypt demonstrates how easy it was for foreigners to become nationalized. The more materialistic the point of view, the less exclusive it would be. Political exclusionist legislation, as established later, would have been out of the question then. According to Herodotus (II, 18), anyone who drank from the Nile was considered an Egyptian. Joseph and Moses were considered full Egyptians. The former even united himself to the daughter of a priest from Heliopolis. . . .[43]

If one replaced the names of Joseph and Moses with those, say, of La Guardia or Einstein, the passage might have been written about the United States!

A third point of comparison between the matriarchal peoples of old and the modern, other-directed mass societies is provided by the "accent on youth." The pre-individual matriarchal people were dark and death-minded. Old age was not the venerable culmination of individual life and achievement, as it is in individualistic-patriarchal societies, but a bridge toward death.* Success and power, therefore, are invested in the last-born, not in the first-born, since the youngest, in Bachofen's words "delays the death of the stock. . . . In the Homeric [patriarchal] world Zeus is supreme in accordance with the law of primogeniture. Hesiod, the poet of gynarchy, on the contrary, makes Zeus the youngest of his brothers. In general, he conceives of the youngest as the most powerful, the founder of world orders."[44]

The dark- and death-mindedness of our society has taken the form of H-bomb apocalypticism, while our "accent on youth" is

---

* That this attitude exists also in post-individual collectivist societies, making "aging" a real problem, is documented in a recent essay by Yonina Talman: "Aging in Israel, a Planned Society," in the *American Journal of Sociology*, November, 1961.

too obvious to need much comment. In the eyes of the other-directed crowd, a man is through long before reaching the solemn age of the patriarchs. Women "delay death" with dyes and diets, and the place of the venerable old lady has been taken by the mummified Junior Miss. In 1960 the tender age of both candidates to the Highest Office in the United States bespoke the voters' faith in youth.

The "accent on youth," for that matter, is characteristic of all post-individual mass societies. The Fascist anthem was *"Giovinezza, giovinezza!"* ("Youth, youth!").

There is a prophetic ring to the conclusion of Bachofen's great work: "The end of political development," he says, "resembles the beginning of human existence. Primeval equality returns at last. Maternal-material existence opens and closes the cycle of human history."

In brief, modern science seems to corroborate what poets have always intuited: that women show the characteristics popularly ascribed to the mass soul or mob spirit.

For it is true that women show a "diminished individualism and variability." And analytic reason, a recent mutation, is more firmly established in men than in women. These are facts of natural evolution.

It is also true that women, during the individualistic phase of human history, and during the transition from the individualistic to the post-individualistic phase, are more repressed, more frustrated, and more alienated than men. This is a fact of cultural evolution.

Group-force induces diminished individualism and variability. It is engendered by, and engenders, emotions, whereas analytic reason is individual and separating. Group-force accelerates, and is accelerated by, repression, frustration, and alienation.

Finally, group-force tends to minimize sexual differences and to make women and men behave alike, and this, in the present circumstances, acts to improve the lot of women. Consequently, a number of similarities between feminine traits and group-force-induced traits become plausible, and a number of parallels can be drawn between our post-individual mass society and the pre-individual matriarchal or matrilinear societies of old.

THREE

In Heaven as on Earth
The Group-Force Time-Vector

The "division of labor" among early mankind is always archetypically conditioned and cannot be explained "from outside," i.e., sociologically. There is no such thing as sexual fitness or unfitness for this or that task. We find inactive men and warrior women, just as we find inactive women and warrior men, and the relation of the group to the powers may be the affair either of men or women.

For the life of the group, the "psychic means of production" are at least of equal importance with the economic. While outward life depends on the one, the equally important inner life, which at the primitive level expresses itself as a relation to the powers, depends on the other. The distribution of these tasks between the sexes and their shifts in correlation are among the essential problems of human history.

ERICH NEUMANN[1]

The affinity between the feminine and the collective seems to have penetrated man's unconscious and to reflect itself in language and art, in myth and faith—creations, all, of the group-force time-vector.

That the social structure of heaven should mirror the social structure on earth seems only too natural. "Whether the god or the goddess is regarded as the head of the divine family is determined by the social organization of human society," G. A. Barton notes. "In matriarchal communities a goddess is the supreme deity, in patriarchal communities, a god."[2]

This seems logical; but in the face of recent depth-psychological and mythological research, it would seem oversimplified. The situation is more complex, but well worth looking into; it is here, at the wellsprings of human consciousness, in the origins of human society, that we find a key to the mystery of the affinities between the feminine and the collective.

The myth of the matriarchate, as revived by Bachofen[3] and Briffault[4] and endorsed by Engels[5] and other socialists, has been exploded by subsequent research in social anthropology. Nor would it square with the theory of sex-balance and group dynamics as proposed in Chapter I. The small hordes of primitives, with an approximately equal number of males and females, could not, like ants or bees, produce dominating, superior females. The male was bound to be bigger and sturdier and, at least to some extent, dominant. But it is in this group-dynamical field, thus delimited, that the study of the relations between the female and the collective becomes fascinating.

That the group-force, in primitive prehistoric societies, was at a maximum, is confirmed by the unanimous testimony of anthropologists, mythologists, and depth-psychologists. "The collective existence of the group stood in the foreground," says Erich Neumann. "Individuality and individual relations between men and women were relatively undeveloped. Early man lived in the middle of this psychological space in which outside and inside, world and man, powers and things, are bound together in an indissoluble unity."[6]

How fantastically modern! Yet this ancient psychological state had to await the most modern one to be fully grasped and understood; for without a deep inner correspondence there can be no reconstruction of a state of mind, just as there can be no successful imitation of a style of art without such inner correspondence. The reversion to the styles of the primitives, so striking in so much of modern art, thus cannot be considered a fad, but as a deep and genuine expression of the adaptation of the post-individualist to the pre-individualist mind.

This collective "psychological space," then, sets the norm. The interrelations between society and the individual are so total that even sickness, for example, is not viewed as an individual fate and failing, but as something disrupting the social order. Sickness among the Australian aborigines "does not have its primary origin in some organic maladjustment," writes Phyllis Kaberry, "but rather in a disturbance of the normal functioning of social relationship. When a cure is not effected, the baramambin postulates the working of an evil force, such as that of the sorcerer who is impeding the normal success of the measures which have been taken. Continued illness leads to further rupture of social relationship."[7]

This unity between the individual and the universe, the one and the all, implies a psychosomatic concept of sickness and health. Any change in nature is coincidental with a change in man himself. Again, how amazingly modern!

The essence of this unity, of this collective, was woman—as bee-like as possible. The shelterer, the nourisher, the life-giver, the priestess and the witch, the medicine woman, the potter of cosmic vessels, the spinner of the threads of life: woman was central; man was marginal. And the projection of this collective was the great mother-goddess who—as is now generally acknowledged—preceded the male god everywhere in the world.

In group-dynamical terms, the primeval mother-goddess— benign, life-giving goddess of fertility, and horrid, blood-dripping, life-devouring demon of night and destruction—is a projection of high growth potential. In her motherly and in her awful aspects she reflects and symbolizes the high birth rate and the high death rate of a population, and the (feminine) character which it engenders and by which it is engendered.

The emergence of individual consciousness breaks this unity. As Hermann Baumann points out in *Das Doppelte Geschlecht,* "Sex-antagonism always reflects a crisis in the relation between the individual and the collectivity."[8]

What is this emergence of individual consciousness? It is the interiorization of tradition, if we want to merge Kahler's and Riesman's terminologies; the split, and the progressive assertion of inside over outside, of reason over fate, of logic against chance, of the one against the many. That this process, this transition, is expressed in mythology by the triumph of the male god over his mother-origin, and, more generally, of the male principle over the female principle, is well-established by now.

For *nous,* mind, and *nomos,* rational law that can be grasped by mind, are masculine; whereas *tyche,* chance or fate, is feminine.

> *I have lifted mine heart to the skies,*
> *I have searched all truths with mine eyes.*
> *But naught more strong*
> *Than Fate have I found . . .*

There is none other Goddess beside
To the altars of whom
No man draweth near, nor hath cried
To her image, nor victim hath died
Averting her doom.
O Goddess more mighty for ill,
Come not upon me
Than in days overpast: for his will
Even Zeus may in no wise fulfill
Unholpen by thee. . . .[9]

Where *nous* rises, there fate must sink and be overcome. And it
is women on earth and goddesses in heaven who stand for fate,
who defend fate; and men, and gods, who rebel. Like Zeus,
when, in the sixteenth book of the Iliad, he looks down on poor
Sarpedon, on the battlefield, where fate has doomed him to fall
at the hands of Patroclus. Zeus was "of two minds whether to
catch him up out of the fight and set him down safe and sound
in the fertile land of Lycia, or let him now fall by the hand of
the son of Menoetius." But the goddess Hera calls him to order:
"Would you snatch a mortal man, whose doom has long been
fated, out of the jaws of death? Do as you will, but we shall
not all of us be of your mind." And Zeus wills as *fate* and the
goddess and the *collective* council of gods wants him to will, and
his son Sarpedon meets his doom.

The fate of fate, the fall of fate from an all-enveloping all-
inclusive reality, to a force, a weight, that can be countered or
offset by gods or by men, by individual free will, is the fate of
woman, the fall of woman, the fall of Eve. The rise of individual consciousness, individuation, thus coincides with the rise
of dualism. This is what Pythagoras means when he says that
the contrast between the One and the Many contains within itself all other contrasts: right and left, male and female, motion
and rest, light and darkness, good and evil.

The more dualistic the world-view of a society, the lower will be the state of its women : secluded, veiled, they are considered the incarnation of evil; whereas societies in which women are integrated and play a prominent role, tend to a unitary world-view, whether as primitive faith in the mother-goddess or as modern materialism.*

In group-dynamical terms, the emergence of individual consciousness, the interiorization of tradition, or the process of individuation, coincides with the shift from a population with high growth potential to a population in a transitional phase of growth, with the emphasis on struggle and fight that this implies.

Only if we consider the goddess as a projection of a pre-individualistic or un-individualistic collectivity, can it become clear why, long after the dawn of consciousness, long after the legend of the matriarchate had gone down into the mythological past, every historical move toward collectivism coincided with the re-emergence of the goddess. The masses remained bound to female deities, whereas the elites—aristocracies, priesthoods, schools —created male gods. In Roman history, Ceres was the protectress of the plebs. The plebeian community, to quote Bachofen, belongs to her, "just as in Athens the assembly of the people is in closest connection with Demeter. Under Ceres' protection, the community sits in council. To the higher, solar [masculine] consecration of the patriciate, the people oppose the inviolability of the primal mother. The plebs enter the state from the feminine-materialistic side."[10]

Class warfare, then, is like a shadow cast on this earth by sex warfare in the remote heavens. Or the rivalry between gods and goddesses is but a projection of the struggle on earth between masses (female) and elites (male).

During the fourth millennium B.C., Semitic tribes infiltrated

---

* In post-individual society, Fate has been replaced by Statistics, a theme that I have treated in a short story, "Delphi Revisited" (*To Whom it May Concern,* New York, Braziller, 1959).

into Babylonia. Coming from the arid plains of Arabia, they were poor, lean, and savage, even if a bit less so than most peoples at that time. Their religion was animalistic, controlled by totems and taboos. Because of the pre-individualist state of their development, their chief deity was a goddess named, variously, Ashtar, Ishtar, Astar, or Ashtart. Ishtar provided water for them in the desert; she led them in battle: but above all, she gave life. She was a goddess of fertility, and many births she assisted when she was benign, and many died when she was hostile.

Then cities were founded: Eridu, Ur, Erech, Lagash. The soil was generous; the population exploded. The communitarian order of the immigrants gave way to one based on private property and slavery. Marduk, a male god of war, became the god of the kings, the priests, and the ruling class: but, as Barton says, "He never displaced the Goddess in the affection of the people. The female principle remained supreme in popular imagination."[11]

To the extent that religion was de-popularized, systematized, and channeled through schools, the female element was pushed out. The priestess, prominent in the early cult, was replaced by the priest in the days when the culture and power of Babylon and Assyria reached their zenith. Rationalization, that is, individualization, was de-feminization; but popular myth, like a collective dream, went its own way. Ishtar's power was unimpaired: though challenged by heroes—Etona, Gilgamesh—she remained "the mistress of the gods." The aristocratic sun-heroes were doomed to wander lonely and ailing into the underworld.

Here, in the underworld, called Aralu, the struggle between the popular-feminine and the aristocratic-masculine principle was even more dramatic.

In the old days, the underworld, like the upper world, was ruled by a queen; in this case, Allatu. When the aristocratic

Marduk pushed Ishtar from the throne in the kings' pantheon, the kings' priests and scribes decided that the matriarchal conditions still prevailing in the underworld were atavistic and that the realm of their dead was to be presided over by a male god as was the realm of their living. Nergal—so they busily inscribed on their tablets—Nergal, the god of the midday sun, of war and of pestilence, was sent down from heaven. With an escort of destructive monsters he forced open the gates of Aralu. The shadows of the dead paled in the glory of his onslaught. All creation trembled with the queen as he faced her and threatened to kill her. She begged for her life. She offered herself to him in marriage. She handed over to him the tablets of wisdom and made him her master and Aralu's.

So wrote the scribes, in their well-thought-out and carefully drawn cuneiforms.

But the people did not care. Year after year, on the popular feast day, when Ishtar went down to Aralu to win back her dead husband, she found there Queen Allatu, unchallenged mistress of the realm, to plead with. For, says Morris Jastrow in *The Religion of Babylonia and Assyria:*

In the popular mind, indeed, despite the influence of theological doctrines, Allatu continued to be more prominent than Nergal. . . . This limitation in the development of the doctrine that elsewhere gave the male principle the supremacy over the female, may be taken as a valuable indication of the counterinfluence exercised by deeply rooted popular beliefs, over the theoretical elaboration of the religion at the hand of the religious guides.[12]

The history of Egypt provides another example. In Egypt, Re, the Sun, was the god of the kings, of the state, and the ruling class, while the people felt drawn toward the worship of Isis and Osiris. The contrast between these two religious themes, according to Breasted, constitutes the main plot of that history. Re reflected the absolute power of the pharaoh at a time

when the people had no will and no rights of their own and were
but tools to drag and hew the boulders for the houses of eternal
rest for the eternal sun king. With the awakening of the people,
the emergence of the common man, Isis and Osiris come into
their own and obscure the sun. The "Osirisation of Re," as
Breasted calls it, has begun. "We see it in the triumph of folk-
religion as opposed to, or contrasted with, the state cult of Re,
which was not unlike an established Church. The supremacy of
Re was a political triumph, that of Osiris, while unquestionably
fostered by an able priesthood probably practising constant propaganda, was a triumph of popular faith among all classes of
society."[13]

The Isis-and-Osiris cult was banned again, and all its traces
were erased, by the solar zeal of Ikhnaton, that "first individuality" of human history, so youthful and charming yet so brutal,
so creative and liberating yet so oppressive, Adonis and Savona-
rola in one, the "criminal of Akhetaton." But his coup could not
have lasting effects, and Isis and Osiris returned, lifted by the
faith of the millions, over the setting sun of a disintegrating
aristocracy.

The Isis-and-Osiris religion is an exaltation of the feminine
principle, a cult of the immortal mother, creating and recreating
a mortal god. Says Bachofen: "Immortal is Isis, mortal her
husband, like the earthly creation which he represents. . . . Isis
precedes Osiris by far in the cult and in the veneration of the
country, which remains notable also later, when the Nile religion
spread over the Roman Empire."[14]

This takes us into a period of proletarianization, of massifica-
tion of the Empire. About ninety per cent of the Roman popu-
lace was made up of freed slaves, many of them imported from
the Orient. Become Roman citizens, they had to be wooed by the
politicians, and in a turmoil of bread and circuses and extrava-
gance and effeminization, the family began to go to pieces.

Divorce became a commonplace, and married couples avoided parenthood. We are in a period of incipient decline of population; which, in Riesman's terminology, engenders an other-directed type of population. That is, the group-force space-vector integrates or takes over the action of the time-vector acting on tradition-directed populations.

But, whether time- or space-vector, the group-force engenders femininity. The cult of Cybele, the Magna Mater of Phrygia, was introduced at about this time (204 B.C.). During the first century B.C. the Egyptian Isis and other Oriental goddesses were welcomed and worshipped by the lower classes. The conservative citizens and the Roman Senate did all they could to stem the tide, but they finally had to yield.

In the struggle between elites and masses, the goddess is, so to speak, a sop to the masses; she is accepted by the elites in order to pacify the masses' needs. The Far-Eastern goddess of mercy had this function of pacifying the popular demand for divine female attributes, just as in the Near East the great mother-goddess who continues to survive is the Virgin Mother.

In the history of the Christian religion, Mariolatry provides another striking example of the coincidence of the female and the mass.

As is well known, Mary's role in the Gospels is meager. It is even surprising that the Mother of the Savior should have so little to say, should deserve so little attention as Mary actually receives. The few passages revealing her relation with Jesus are markedly unharmonious.

Apparently quite unaware of his mission, she—*not* the father —scolds the twelve-year-old who is tarrying at the temple (Luke 2 : 48-50) : "Son, why hast thou thus dealt with us? Behold, thy father and I have sought thee sorrowing. And he said unto them, How is it that ye sought me? Wist ye not that I must

be about my Father's business? And they understood not the
saying which he spake unto them."

Still more rudely he deals with her at the marriage feast at
Cana (John 2 : 1-4) where, at her innocent remark, "They have
no wine," he bursts out, "Woman, what have I to do with thee?"
Nor does he seem eager to have anything to do with her when,
advised (Luke 8 : 20-21) : "Thy mother and thy brethren stand
without, desiring to see thee," he remains cold to their desire, indeed he ignores their existence. "And he answered and said unto
them : My mother and brethren are these which hear the word of
God, and do it." In an analogous way he rejects, according to
Luke (11 : 27-28), the idea that his mother is "blessed" or in
any way preferred by God to other women: "A certain woman
of the company lifted up her voice and said unto him, Blessed is
the womb that bare thee, and the paps which thou hast sucked.
But he said, Yea, rather blessed are they that hear the word of
God, and keep it."

One single passage in the Gospels, the beginning of Luke
(1 : 46-48), does honor to Mary: "My soul doth magnify the
Lord, and my spirit hath rejoiced in God my Saviour. For he
hath regarded the low estate of his handmaiden: for behold,
from henceforth all generations shall call me blessed." Here is
the root of the cult of Mary the Great Mother. What a startling
coincidence that the first announcement of the cult of the mother
goddess should also be the first Christian communist manifesto!
"He hath scattered the proud in the imagination of their hearts.
He hath put down the mighty from their seats, and exalted them
of low degree. He hath filled the hungry with good things, and
the rich he hath sent empty away" (Luke 8 : 51-53).*

The cult of Mary becomes reality when, with the conversion
of Constantine, Christianity becomes the religion of the masses

---

* This, incidentally, is the almost literal repetition of the prophecy of a
woman, the poetess Hannah, in the Old Testament.

and, as Cardinal Newman put it : "The spirit of the world was poured into the Church."

A flock of believers trekked into Arabia from Thrace. To give thanks at the end of their wandering, the children gathered wood, and the fathers kindled the fire, and the women kneaded dough to make cakes for Mary the new Queen of Heaven, and they poured out libations. As of old through Jeremiah, thus said the Lord through Epiphanius : "Behold mine anger and my fury shall be poured out upon this place." The worship of Mary is anathematized in the twenty-fourth of the Panarion's eighty heresies, where Epiphanius states : "Let Mary be had in honor, but let the Lord be worshiped."

But the official church could not stem the torrent. It swept the imagination of the masses. The goddess dominated the totalitarian-collectivist phase of Christianity embodied in the Catholic Church.

Strikingly, the wave set out from the East, from the lands that were, before and after, the lands of communalism and collectivism, as opposed to the more individualistic West. The lower we descend on the social ladder, from the hierarchy to the anonymous masses, the higher rings the praise of the most holy Mother of God. "Light of my darkened soul, my hope, protection, and refuge. I thank thee that thou hast enabled me to be a partaker of the Body and Blood of Thy dear Son. Enlighten the eyes of my heart. Quicken me. Give me tears of repentance and thanksgiving." Thus prayed the Russian crowds.

The West kept wary for a while. To awaken fully to the charm of the goddess, it needed the push of a collective action : the people's holy wars. Mass movement, collective hysteria bursting forth in pogroms and children's crusades, with the lowest elements of society swept to the surface and criminals set at large and the poor awaiting the Mother of Pity : this is the background that sets in relief the figure of St. Bernard (1090–

1153), bathed in luminous love of the Virgin, whose cult at that time rises to its acme.

It also happens that the women of this world gained in power and influence at that time. Men's lives were shortened by the stress of war and the excess of luxuries imported from the East, and capable widows remained in charge of castles, fortunes, and sons. Provençal poetry of the twelfth century is a celebration and idealization of this type of woman: elegant, well-read, experienced; a woman who knows "the laws of the court of love," socially and economically independent, and open to easy courtship; yet endowed by the poets with divine qualities.

Otto Weininger ascribes the emergence of this type of dominant woman to an increase in the hermaphroditic birth rate, which he believes to occur periodically throughout history.

"Is it not striking," he asks, "that the activities for women's emancipation seem to be distributed in world history in constant, always equal, intervals? During the tenth century, during the fifteenth and sixteenth, and now again in the nineteenth and twentieth, there has been undoubtedly a much greater number of emancipated women and a far stronger women's movement than in the intermediate periods." And this he ascribes "to an impressive periodicity," with which "more hermaphrodites, more intermediate forms, are born into this world at certain regular intervals. An analogous periodicity can be observed among animals."[15]

This is an interesting observation, though hard to prove or disprove. There remains the fact that, among animals, as we have pointed out in Chapter I, shifts in the sex balance and structure in individuals are connected with group-dynamical changes. Although population statistics are scarce for two of the three periods cited by Weininger, we feel tempted to associate the emergence of a dominant type of woman—with or without incidence of "intermediate forms"—with a shift from a transitional-growth to an incipient-decline society :* in the wake of expansion and urbanization at the time of the Crusades; in the wake of the intellectual conquests and commercial expansion of the Renaissance; and, obviously, in our own day. That such shifts in the population dynamics may occur periodically, like outbreaks in the animal kingdom, seems likely. More than real shifts, however, they ought to be considered as incipient or potential shifts. The changes they may make in the sex balance are superficial indeed. Thus, in the Middle Ages, a small number of chatelaines were affected, but not the common woman.

But to return to the cult of Mary, we find it abolished and anathematized by the Protestant Reformation.

Protestantism, in its origin, obviously is an individualistic revolt. It rescued the individual, restoring the direct contact between each soul and its creator and doing away with intermediaries—whether priest or mother-goddess—between God and the people.

Martin Luther calls woman "a stupid vessel" and sends her sternly back to the place she occupied in the mind of St. Paul: for "man is higher and better than she; for the regiment and dominion belong to man as the head and master of the house; as St. Paul says elsewhere: Man is God's honor and God's image. Item: Man does not exist for the sake of woman, but woman exists for the sake of man and hence there shall be this difference, that a man shall love his wife but never be subject to her, but the wife shall honor and fear her husband, in all obedience and awe."[16]

If in subsequent centuries the emancipation of women has been achieved primarily in Protestant countries, while it is still

*According to Karl Bucher *(Die Frauenfrage im Mittelalter),* the numerical superiority of women in the Middle Ages was far greater than today, varying from ten per cent to as much as twenty-five per cent!

badly lagging in Catholic countries, this is due to other developments, which, though initially rooted in religion, or at any rate
connected with the religious situation, have since gone their own
way. To this we shall return later. For the present it may suffice
to point out that the cult of the mother-goddess is limited to the
collectivist-authoritarian phase of Christianity, that Mary is the
goddess of the masses, whereas individualist Christianity, elite
Christianity, does not recognize her.

However, to study religions merely under the mechanistic cri-
terion of whether their pantheon or divine family is male- or
female-dominated, would not do justice to the subject. The relations between mortals and their gods are more subtle than that.

Every religion has a powerful collectivist component, as
emphasized by Durkheim,[17] Smith,[18] and others. "Social co-
operation is needed to surround the unveiling of things sacred
and of supernatural beings with solemn grandeur," according to
Malinowski.[19] The inviolacy, transmission, and conservation of
sacred tradition entails collectiveness of performance.

Nevertheless there are religions which stress the value of the
individual who fulfills himself in contemplative isolation rather
than in collective rites. Hermitism—whether Buddhist or Christian, Eastern or Western—is wholly masculine. But there are
other cults that engender, and are engendered by, collective
frenzy. Let us see what role is played by women in this latter
category.

Take the prototype of this sort of religion: the religion of
girl-faced Dionysus—Bacchus, with the flowing locks. The cult
of Dionysus is the cult of unity of body and soul, of the spiri-
tualization of the flesh.

Divine Demeter—
Earth is she, name her by which name thou wilt;

She upon dry food nurtureth mortal men:
Then follows Semele's Son: to match her gift
The cluster's flowing draught he found, and gave
To mortals, which gives rest from grief to men . . .
Woe-worn, soon as the vine's stream filleth them . . .[20]

This is communion of bread and wine, of body and blood-soul. The cult of Dionysus is classless:

From all alike he claims his due of honor.
. . . On the high, on the low doth his bounty bestow.[21]

And thus he creates a typical mass psychology, including even panic:

Somewhat of Ares' dues he shares withal:
Hosts, harness-clad, in ranks arrayed, sometimes
Are thrilled with panic ere a spear be touched:
This too is a frenzy Dionysus sends. . . .[22]

As a creator of mass psychology, as a social leveler and emancipator of the servile classes, Dionysus was favored by tyrants whose power rested on popular enthusiasm rather than on the reasoned consent of elite councils.

But the first and foremost followers of this new god who invaded Greece from Asia, and Rome from Greece were women.

Asiatic women, who have followed him, make up the chorus that glorifies his virtues and powers.

It is the women that he drives from their Theban homes:

Feigning a Bacchic rapture, and rove wild
Over wooded hills, in dance honoring
Dionysus, this new God—who e'er he be.[23]

Before being overpowered by Bacchus and yielding to his madness, Pentheus has to don women's clothes.

And sixteen matrons were Dionysus' priestesses at Elis.

The impact of the Dionysian religion on the Old World is throughout feminine-materialistic, says Bachofen. And his hold on women is greater, just because women are more *communal*, readier to tear down the barriers between individual and individual.

The community of Pythagoreans, likewise, exalts the feminine principle, and the performance of women in this movement is of the utmost importance. The list of Pythagorean women includes Lasthenia of Messenia and Axiothea of Phlius; the five daughters of Diodorus; Gemina, mother and daughter; Amphiclea; Pamphila of Epidaurus, and half a dozen more.

Pythagoras appears, says Bachofen, as protector and advocate of the feminine sex, as defender of women's rights and inviolability, as exalter of their position in family and State. The oppression of women is presented to men as a sin. Equal vocation, and the equal dignity of the masculine and feminine mind are emphasized throughout his teaching—which also prescribes community of life and of the possessions of the group![24]

But here we are on the borderline between the mythical-unconscious and the philosophical-conscious, which we do not wish to transgress in this already overlong chapter. All we intend to do here is to establish a trend, which has been identified and documented by numerous experts. It may be enough to mention, in conclusion, the enormous importance of women in all celebrations of mysteries, from the Egyptian to the Eleusinian to the Roman. The deity at the center of these mysteries is always female: Demeter, Kore, Cybele, Isis, the Great Mother;* women are part of the ecstatic crowd; and women perform as priestesses, impersonating the goddesses in sacred dramas.

As the human collective tends to fall back on a female deity,

* Mithra constitutes the exception that confirms the rule.

so does the divine collective, amazingly often, fall into female components. We think of those deities who do not appear or act singly, who often have no personal names, no distinct traits, but sing and speak and war and weave in groups : such as the Muses or Graces, who, daughters of reason, mothers of art, inspire in man a desire for beauty and harmony; such as the Erinyes, or Furies, daughters of Fate, mothers of Natural Law, with their serpent-hair and fire-breath and blood-teeth, who benight and destroy; such as the Moirai or Parcae or Norms, who spin and order and cut the thread of human life. And all the other goddesses of birth and fate, all-wise mothers or pretty lasses, with pale cheeks and bewitching eyes, attired in white, their ethereal bodies almost transparent, as they people the moonlit Slavonic nights. And many others! the Valkyries, who rule men's battles and convey the heroes to Valhalla; the nymphs, the swan-maidens, or the Pleiades.

Group goddesses are familiar to all imaginations; group gods are not. This fact was noted by Erich Neumann, who has this comment: "Their plurality usually indicates that they belong to a state of the human consciousness prior to the configurative phase in which they appear as goddesses; or else they may be figures that, superseded by the dominant gods, have regressed to a more primitive and anonymous, preconfigurative state."[25]

Creations of the unconscious group mind, they are groups, and they are female.

To sum up: The goddess belongs to the masses; the god, to the elites.

The frenzy of collective rites appeals to women more than to men who find spiritual fulfillment also in isolation.

Divine groups, collective deities, consist of female rather than male components.

This much is implicit, or even stated explicitly in dozens of scholarly works, but scattered here and there, not focused upon anywhere as a central thesis. We look at it, not as an isolated, more or less interesting fact, but in the context of the Birds and the Bees, and Women and Crowds. We see in it one more—and an important—manifestation of the basic affinity between the collective and the female; which, if it can be demonstrated—and by now we are rather sure it can—may change our whole outlook with regard to the "feminine revolution" and the "crisis of the family" which we are facing today.

FOUR

La Lingua Batte Dove
Il Dente Duole

*To sum up, we can say that the fundamental gram-
matical categories, universal to all human languages, can be understood only with reference to
the pragmatic* Weltanschauung *of primitive man,
and that, through the use of language, the barbar-
ous primitive categories must have deeply influ-
enced the later philosophies of mankind.*

BRONISLAW MALINOWSKI[1]

The Italians say: *"La lingua batte dove il dente duole."* La *lingua* is "the tongue," in the physiological sense, which "hits," or "touches," "where the tooth aches." But both tongue and toothache may be metaphorical. The tongue may be understood to mean language or speech; and the toothache, trouble in general. With reference to the individual, the proverb then means that one always comes to speak of one's troubles somehow. With reference to humanity at large, it may mean that if there is a deep-seated complex of ideas, it should reflect itself somehow in the history and evolution of language, which creates and is created by the social relationships underlying such complexes.

If the affinity between the feminine and the collective is as deep seated in the human mind and in the human group as we assume it to be, we should find it reflected in language, in every language, in the history of language.

Translated into linguistic terms, the affinity between the female and the collective becomes an affinity between the feminine gender and the plural or collective.

Going back, way back, to the origins of language, to proto-Aryan, the very first language that is known to have been spoken in prehistoric times somewhere in Asia, we find indeed that the feminine is the collective!

The noun indicating, for example, an animal, was not characterized, in proto-Aryan times, by any specific ending or affix or formans: *ekuos* was a horse in general, a "horsish being"; *ulquos* was a wolf in general, a "wolfish being." In contrast to *one* such being, *ekua* (nominative and accusative plural) indicated a lot of horses, *ulqui*, a group of wolves.

73

May we assume that it indicated the lair, with the she-wolf and the cubs, while *ulquos* was the lone he-wolf who brought back the meat? This is just a wild guess; but the fact is that *ulqui* became the she-wolf, and that the transition from the collective to the individual-feminine has been studied and documented by glottologists. In the process, the feminine ending, or formans, of an object-denoting noun—usually vocalic and bright —was dissociated from its original sexual implication; although, as Bruggmann points out in his *Grundriss*,[2] such an ending, in turn, finished by coloring sexually the meaning of the noun to which it was affixed. This becomes most obvious in words like the Greek *helios, hypnos, selenae, nyx, hygieia,* or the Latin *amor, victoria, pax,* or the German *Sonne, Mond, Minne,* which have been transformed into mythological personalities of one sex or another.

Thus the feminine form was born of the collective. Conversely, the collective is born of the feminine. This, one might say, is a universal fact. Johannes Schmidt tells the story in *Die Pluralbildung der Indogermanischen Neutra.*[3] Speaking of masculine nouns, which have a neutral plural ending, he points out that these plurals originally were singulars, as is evidenced by the fact that they call for a singular verbal predicate form in Sanskrit and also in Greek. This, he says, proves that originally these neuter plurals were collective feminine singulars. The same phenomenon has been observed in Arabic, where such plurals, originating in a feminine collective singular, are known as *plurales fracti.* The *pluralis fractus* differs from the normal plural in that the latter indicates a plurality of individuals, whereas the former indicates a collective. The Arabic *plurales fracti* are really singulars with a collective meaning, often approaching abstract meaning; and they are always feminine. Similar feminine collectives can be found in Egyptian and in Hebrew.

The phenomenon repeats itself in the modern Romance languages. Take, for instance, those Italian nouns which form two plurals, such as *braccio, dito, frutto,* or *legno.* Such concepts as "this dish of fruit," or "the wood in front of the fireplace," ready-made before our inner eye, in which the single component, fruit or log, has lost all individuality, are expressed through the "collective" or feminine form: *la legna* or *le legna, la frutta* or *le frutta.* At the same time, there exists the regular masculine form, describing an addition of individuals. "Each of the fruits on this tree is worm-eaten"; "each piece of furniture was made of a different kind of wood:" *I frutti, i legni.* Now, what has become a feminine form in modern Italian was, in some cases, simply the regular plural form of the Latin neuter noun; for example, *lignum, ligna,* which became *legna.* It is interesting to note, however, that not all Latin neuter nouns have conserved their regular plural form, which is identical with the feminine, but only those conveying the idea of a collectivity, while the others have been transformed into masculines. Moreover, new cases have been added: nouns that were not neuter in Latin: *le frutta, le mura, le braccia.*

An analogous fate has femininized the Latin *folia* (neuter plural), the leaves, collectively, the foliage; in French, *la feuille.* Likewise, the Latin neuter plural *fortia* has become in Italian *la forza* (feminine), and the Latin neuter plural *gaudia* has become a feminine singular in French, *la joie,* and in Italian, *la gioia.*

As we have already indicated, the affinity between the collective and the feminine is not restricted to the so-called Aryan or Indo-European group of languages. Morris Jastrow finds the same thing true of the Semitic languages. "It should be noted," he writes, "that at a certain stage in the development of the Semitic languages, the feminine is hardly distinguishable from the plural and collective."[4]

So this is one aspect of the problem, where linguistic development reflects an association that is deeply embedded in the psycho-bio-social life of the species.

There are other aspects.

Halfway between the masculine or neuter plural on the one hand, and the feminine singular on the other, we find the noun denoting a collective. Examples are the Greek *phratria,* "brotherhood," *ekklaesia,* "popular assembly," *gerousia,* "the council of the ancient"; or the Latin *familia,* "the domestic community," *juventa,* "youth"; the Lithuanian *sargyba,* "society"; all the Latin words ending in *-udo* (as *multitudo*) or *-itas* (*communitas*) or *-tio* (*natio*); or the German words ending in *-schaft* (*Gemeinschaft*) or *-heit* (*Gesamtheit*) : they are all feminine.

With the feminine endings must have been associated, as far back as Proto-Aryan times, abstract meaning, feminine meaning, and, generally, collective meaning, explains Bruggmann in *Grundriss,* cited above.

This association can be traced even in modern English, which has done away with gender distinction to a sweeping extent: a country or nation, in English, is feminine. We speak of England and *her* Empire, of Russia and what *she* has achieved in science: an echo from the times when the names of all nations and countries were feminine—Greece, Italy, Gaul, etc.

But "she" is also a city, a church, a college, a government, insofar as it stands for the community of its members. The concept of any community is feminine in English.

From the collective abstract we pass to the abstract *tout court:* the adjective abstract denoting a general quality, such as beauty, wisdom, kindness, or wickedness. Such abstracts are feminine, too, in the Indo-European as well as in the Semitic group of languages. Where mythology has personified such abstracts, they are represented by female deities; in daily speech they may be applied to a woman : a woman may be addressed as "Beauty," for example. In German, *Schönheit* may be a woman, whereas it would be rather queer to call a man that.

The typical, the generic, the non-individual, thus, are associated in our minds, and therefore in our languages, with the feminine, no less than the collective.

The evolution of language is like the evolution of life. From the undifferentiated howl of the monkey pack, it goes through a long, infinitely long and complex process of differentiation (individualization) until, at a certain point, the opposite trend sets in, and language tends to simplification and streamlining (depersonalization). The rich, differentiated language then remains "archaic," like Russian today, or, to some extent, German, while the most modern, the most evolved of Western languages, English, approximates, in more than one aspect, the oldest and preindividualist one, Chinese.

It should be noted that in this phase of the evolution of any language, as it strives, from a multiplicity of forms, for unification and simplicity, it is the plural that first abolishes the difference in gender, just as the mass merges male and female, absorbing alike the strength of the one and the weakness of the other.

When we were very young, English students were taught to enlarge their vocabulary as far as possible, to articulate their syntax, to enrich their speech and writing, to enhance, in this way, their personality and put it forward at its fullest and best. Today, students are still taught the fine shades and rich nuances of classical English, but they learn them the way they learn Latin and Greek. Life today calls for a different language : a language that responds to the pressures of democracy, technology, standardization, and internationalization.

The large, semi-literate masses that make up the majority
of our readers and listeners, exact simple texts.

The exigencies of the electronic machine age, which is only
beginning today, increasingly pervade our speaking, writing,
and thinking habits, forcing our statements into a form which
not only will make them understandable to large masses, but
suitable to be fed to the computer.

The shrinking of the world community, the intensification
of international communications, demand phrases that are easily translatable from one language into another—even by machines—or that draw on a small stock of roots common to
several languages and are understandable even without trans-
lation.

We are just at the beginning of this development, but its effects on modery poetry and fiction are already unmistakable.
The de-personalization, de-individualization of language is, of
course, just one more aspect of the de-individualization of modern society in general.

What is the role played by women in this development?

When we look at a page of modern prose or at a poem, we
can usually tell whether it has been written by a man or by a
woman. We may guess wrong, for there are women who write
in a "masculine" way and men who write in a "feminine" way.
But there is a difference between these two ways of writing, a
stylistic difference, a difference in language. Today, one might
say, women writers, on the whole, are wordier than men; they
use more adjectives, are gentler, but also more florid; they seem
to react more consciously, and more self-consciously, to the im-
poverishing trend of the times. Often it seems as if they wanted
to cover up, with a rich form, some deficiency in substance. The
"masculine" way of writing, today, is more terse, more com-
pact. It has more striking power.

Take the following passage by Aldous Huxley:

"But your things are good, Helmholtz." "Oh, as far as they go."
Helmholtz shrugged his shoulders. "But they go such a little way.
They aren't important enough, somehow. I feel I could do something much more important. Yes, and more intense, more violent.
But what? What is there more important to say? And how can one
be violent about the sort of things one's expected to write about?
Words can be like X-rays, if you use them properly—they'll go
through anything. You read and you're pierced. That's one of the
things I try to teach my students—how to write piercingly. But
what on earth's the good of being pierced by an article about a
Community Sing, or the latest improvement in scent organs? Besides, can you make words really piercing—you know, like the very
hardest X-rays—when you're writing about that sort of thing? Can
you say something about nothing? That's what it finally boils down
to. I try and I try. . . ."[5]

Let me try to translate this into "feminine" language:

"I really like your writings, Helmholtz," Bernard said, looking at
him admiringly. "I am fond of them." "I am far from satisfied,"
Helmholtz answered, shrugging his broad shoulders. "Maybe they
are not bad," he went on to explain, "but that is not enough. I feel
I have more important things within me, somehow. I feel I could do
something much more consequential. My heart pulls and aches as
though it wanted to burst. So intense I feel, so violent. But for
some reason I am unable to give expression to this violence, to this
intensity. For what should I say? How can I clothe in a garb of
violence and intensity the unviolent and slack subject matter I am
supposed to deal with? Words can be piercing like X-rays, you
know, if you know how to use them propertly. They'll reveal the
innermost hidden truths. You read and you feel exposed to the
marrow. This, incidentally, is one of the things I've always tried to
teach my students: how to penetrate with words, how to write
piercingly. But, you see, when you are tied down to meaningless
topics, like Community Sings or the latest improvement in scent
organs, it is rather difficult to be penetrating. These matters just
won't pierce, no matter how you dress them up, no matter how

sharply you formulate them. For it's simply impossible to say something about nothing. That is the real crux of the problem."

I hope Mr. Huxley will forgive me these weird doings. I have tried to weaken the bone structure of his prose. To unmuscle it. To make it a bit feelier and flabbier. Now it does sound more as though it had been written by a woman.

Huxley's words are indeed "piercing." With the few that will fit into one short paragraph he manages to express the plight of the modern writer, the hollowness of all the "skillful writing" that goes under the name of modern fiction or poetry.

Compare his passage to the following one by a woman, Simone de Beauvoir, also on writing. The passage, which is both intelligent and very sensitive, runs over many pages. And it *is* flabbier. It does manage to say, if not something about nothing, certainly a lot more about a lot less:

It is natural enough for woman to attempt escape from this world where she often feels slighted and misunderstood; but one regrets only that she does not venture upon the audacious flights of a Gérard de Nerval, an Edgar Allan Poe. There are many good reasons for her timidity. To please is her first care; and often she fears she will be displeasing as a woman from the mere fact that she writes; the term *bluestocking,* though threadbare, continues to have disagreeable connotations; she lacks, further, the courage to be displeasing as a writer. The writer of originality, unless dead, is always shocking, scandalous; novelty disturbs and repels. Woman is still astonished and flattered at being admitted to the world of thought, of art—a masculine world. She is on her best behavior; she is afraid to disarrange, to investigate, to explode; she feels she should seek pardon for her literary pretensions through her modesty and good taste. She relies on the sure values of conformity; she gives literature precisely that personal tone which is expected of her, reminding us that she is a woman by a few well-chosen graces, affectations, and preciosities. All this helps her excel in the production of best-sellers; but we must not look to her for adventuring along strange ways. . . . Woman exhausts her courage dissipating mirages, and she stops in terror at the threshold of reality. . . . We are still too preoccupied with clearly seeing the facts to try to penetrate the shadows beyond that illuminated circle. "Women never go beyond appearances," said a writer to me. It is true enough. Still amazed at being allowed to explore the phenomena of this world, they take inventory without trying to discover meanings. . . ."[6]

"Masculinizing" four pages of this prose, I would say:

Women writers project themselves where men writers come to grips with the universe. Women writers embroider where men writers sculpt.

Obviously this procedure is not fair. I am exaggerating. But the two passages speak for themselves.

I do not want to suggest in any way that this difference is "biologically conditioned," nor that it is constant. At other times it may have manifested itself in other ways. The only "constant" is the fact that there *is* a difference between masculine and feminine speech. It has been studied and documented, not so much by sociologists, nor by the many men and women who have written books about women, but by the glottologists, in highly specialized and not generally accessible, but nonetheless fascinating, essays, books, and symposia. It has been studied not so much with reference to our own society, as concerning ancient languages, from Sanskrit to Scythian; or the dialects within certain linguistic families, such as Bantu or the Rumanian shepherds' speech; or the languages of the American Indians, from Chiquito to Yana; and, most strikingly, among the indigenous populations of the Caribbean islands, who possess two distinct languages, one for men and one for women.

The tendencies to differ are various, and at times are apparently conflicting. But the differences are always reducible to terms of social context.

Professor Carlo Tagliavini sums them up in his excellent
essay on the modifications of language in the speech of women.[7]

Women's speech tends to be more conservative, more archaic
than men's, and this particularly in societies where the women
live a more cloistered and secluded life than the men, whose
professional activities keep them in contact with other groups.
This "archaicizing" tendency was observed by Plato among
Greek women, by Cicero among Romans, and by modern glottologists all over the world—especially with regard to the conservation of dialects, which, generally, survive more intact in
the mouths of women.

At the same time, however, women's speech, distant from the
stabilizing influence of schools and written literature, tends to
precede masculine speech in certain types of phonetic innovation and neologisms, which may arise from many different
causes and situations, ranging from sexual taboos to baby talk.
Such innovations, at any rate, are stubbornly resisted by the
male population and by the upper classes, until, at last, they are
generally taken over by the evolutionary process.

Thus the language of women—except in cases where the
trend is consciously or self-consciously reversed and overcom-
pensated, as in our own time—is the language of the masses.

Take a few examples. In the classical Hindu theater, men generally spoke in Sanskrit, women—even heroines—in Pakrit.
Sanskrit was the language of gods, kings, lords and Brahmans,
whereas the "natural" Prakrit was the language of the lower
castes. Some exceptional high-caste women were able to speak
Sanskrit, while *all* lower-caste men spoke Pakrit. According to
Jesperson:

The difference between the two "languages" is merely social or
"caste." The two ways of speaking constitute two layers of one
and the same language: one of which is superior, more ceremonious
and somewhat stiffer: the other, lowlier, more natural and less

forced; and this free, or should we say, negligent, way of speaking
is the only one recognized in women. The distance between the two
languages is perhaps no greater than that between the speech of a
judge and that of a haberdasher in a modern novel; or than the
difference between the parlance of Juliet, in Shakespeare, and that
of her nurse; and if all women, including those we consider the
drama's "heroines," speak the language of the lower social strata,
we may look for the reason in the fact that women's social position
was so inferior that she had to be placed on the same level with the
lower castes and could not possibly share in higher education, including refined speech, which remained a privilege of a small group
of distinguished men."[8]

Tagliavini cites another example: in Yiddish, "masculine"
language contains a great many more Hebrew elements than
"feminine" language. It can even be claimed that Yiddish made
its way through the world thanks to the women especially.
Many ritualistic texts in Yiddish were written for women who
had not studied Hebrew. In fact, in some parts of Eastern
Europe, Yiddish is known under the name of *Weiberdeutsch*—
"women's German"!

Let me mention one more author, also quoted by Tagliavini,
from whose observations on the Yana Indians we might draw
some general conclusions. Most words, says Edward Sapir,
have "the full or male form and the reduced or female form."
Gender, incidentally, in Yana, as in many other primitive languages, is subjective, not objective. The feminine form of a
word is used by women speaking to women, by women speaking
to men, and by men speaking to women, three times as frequently as the masculine form, which is used only by men speaking to men.

In the great majority of cases the female forms can be best explained as abbreviated forms which in origin had nothing to do with
sex, but which are specialized female applications or reduced forms
suggested by the phonetic and morphologic economy of the lan-

guage. Possibly the reduced, female forms constitute a conventional symbolism of the less considered or ceremonious status of women in the community. Men, in dealing with men, speak fully and deliberately. Where women are concerned, one prefers a clipped style of utterance![9]

Tagliavini notes the same tendency in Chiquito, an indigenous language of Bolivia. "We have seen that also the Chiquito system, however complicated relatively, follows a well-established principle: that feminine language innovates and simplifies grammatical forms."[10]

If the English, especially the American, language today shows this unmistakable tendency to "innovate and simplify grammatical forms"—by cutting down on syntax, simplifying structure, abolishing subordinate clauses, eliminating Latinisms, avoiding "sixty-four-dollar" words in favor of Germanic or Anglo-Saxon monosyllables, introducing slang, simplifying spelling, etc.—we are justified in saying that our language is getting *feminized* as it is getting *collectivized.* The fine, rich, flexible style of some of our women writers and poetesses is not authentic, feminine language, but a self-conscious reaction to a trend felt strongly within and without. These few women writers among us are like the fine Hindu ladies who speak Sanskrit rather than Pakrit: a marginal, if admirable, phenomenon.

In examining the problem of language and sex—or rather, in indicating some possible lines of research—we have distinguished an objective and a subjective aspect. The objective aspect concerns *gender* and *number* in the evolution of language; here the affinity between the collective and the feminine has been documented as a universal fact. The subjective aspect of the problem concerns the distinction—equally universal, though differing in its manifestations according to different social contexts—between a masculine and a feminine language; and, without wanting to force the issue, without undue generalizations, we feel encouraged to conclude that feminine language is closer to the language of the masses, and that the depersonalization or collectivization of language and its femininization go together.

FIVE

Women and the Face
of the Crowd

. . . When I was in America I for the first time travelled pretty much all the time in an airplane and when I looked at the earth I saw all the lines of cubism made at a time when not any painter had ever gone up in an airplane. I saw there on the earth the mingling lines of Picasso, coming and going, developing and destroying themselves. I saw the simple solutions of Braque, I saw the wandering lines of Masson, yes I saw and once more I knew that a creator is contemporary, he understands what is contemporary when the contemporaries do not yet know it, but he is contemporary and as the twentieth century is a century which sees the earth as no one has ever seen it, the earth has a splendor that it never has had. . . .

GERTRUDE STEIN[1]

A long time ago, when I was still a small child, I saw a picture in an illustrated magazine that I shall never forget. It was a montage, contrived by an experimental photographer who wanted to discover the face of the "typical American."

He took a hundred pictures, to this end. Bankers from Manhattan and planters from the South; coal miners in Pennsylvania and farmers in New England; cowboys in Texas, dairymen in Wisconsin; salesmen, office boys, ministers and bartenders. Their pictures—small—framed the large page of the magazine. The center of the page offered a strange sight. All hundred pictures, enlarged so that each face should occupy exactly the same space, were mounted one on top of the other. All these different, not-quite-coinciding nose ridges, cheekbones, eyebrows, and lips, blended into the blurred outlines of a new face: a long aquiline nose, thin, shapely lips, high cheekbones, a sad and serious countenance, however unfocused. To emphasize his discovery, the artist adumbrated long black flowing hair, adorned with a feather. The face of the "typical" American, as it emerged from the superimposition of a hundred faces, was the face of America, an Indian face.

I don't remember whether the face was supposed to be male or female; there wouldn't have been much difference anyway, and I guess nobody could tell.

Nor do I know how much intention, how much tricky arranging went into the montage, and the page has been lost long since. But the result must have been, to some extent, authentic, and it impresses me today more than ever. For it demonstrates

graphically, laying it open before our eyes, how great is the
force of surrounding, of "air," of collectivity; and how limited
is the strength of the individual.

I should like to propose a variant to this experiment. Instead
of taking faces separately, "the people," on a country-wide
basis, take a crowd: a crowd tensely listening to the harangue
of a campaigning candidate; a crowd storming the gates of a
Southern prison where a Negro is being held to prevent his being lynched; a crowd cramming the avenues of a metropolis
at noon, streaming from offices and shops.

If, when you take "people," as in the first experiment, you
obtain an Indian face—a projection of the group-force time-
vector, for there is history behind this "face," accumulated life
experience—what you may get when you take the "crowd" is a
feminine face, a projection of the group-force space-vector, less
distinctly marked, smoother, even if wrinkled, softer, less developed, than man's.

Artists painting crowds—crowds in panic, battle throngs,
revolutionary masses, humanity in the throes of doomsday—
would seem to have sensed this. Just so they have intuited mathematical laws, expressed analytical functions they did not
"know" in their abstract, pure forms.

To see, and represent, a crowd as a crowd is not so simple
as one might think. Children and primitives do not "see"
crowds. It requires some degree of "individuation"; one has to
set oneself up as an individual, separate, to perceive the crowd
as a crowd.

How to represent a crowd has to be learned over again by
each new art. Think of the straggly crowds in the early movies:
Dreyer's "The Passion of Joan of Arc," for example. It is an
absolute masterpiece in the representation of the individual both
as individual and symbol—as in primitive art; but the crowd

here is a skimpy, rough and spotty job. No flow, no *Gestalt*. Not really a crowd. Look, in comparison, at the latest cyclo-ramic crowds, in, let us say, "War and Peace," or "Ben-Hur."

A director might test the reality of his crowds by repeating the feat of that experimental photographer: mounting all the faces. If the result is a woman's face, the crowd is right. If not, the crowd is no crowd.

Technical progress, one might object. The early Dreyer did not have the technical means for the realistic representation of a real crowd. But the means come when the concept is ready. They always do.

They did in painting. Here the story is the same—with a much greater emphasis on the maturation of concept and much less emphasis on the development of means.

There are no crowds in primitive painting.

An evangelistary of Emperor Otto III of the ninth century[2] is decorated with miniatures, one of them depicting Christ's Entry into Jerusalem. The "crowd" hailing the Savior is represented by three little men. That is all. The emphasis is on Jesus, on his entering Jerusalem. The crowd is incidental, unfocused, unreal.

The development of sacred art from that time to the sixteenth century can be seen as a process leading from a symbolic interpretation to a narrative description. That is, from a representation that emphasizes and interprets the universal-symbolic content of a scene to one that presents it as a unique happening and describes it as vividly as possible. This process increasingly includes *people,* who characterize and localize the scene without adding anything to the content, to the action represented.

These people, at first, were few and timid. They might be two, three little men, as in the Ottonian evangelistary. They might be noblemen and high dignitaries of the Church, portraits of individuals, evidently, like those in the frescoes in the Sistine

Chapel, who represent the people witnessing sacred happenings of the Old Testament and the New. Presumably the painters thought only members of the upper classes worthy to stand for humanity as a whole. But these are not crowds; and they lack female depth.

The crowd as a crowd in artistic representation comes from Italy, the place where painting, as early as the first decade of the fourteenth century, had reached the highest level of development, and the individual was capable of considering himself as set off, separate from the "masses." The earliest representation of a real crowd, perhaps, is to be found in Duccio's "Virgin in Majesty" in the Cathedral of Siena (1308–11).

Among the panels there is one on the back of the altar, "The Entry of Christ into Jerusalem," which is worth comparing with the one in the above-mentioned evangelistary. Instead of the crowd being represented by three forlorn little men, we now have a pushing, thronging, flowing mass on which Christ floats toward the town from whence another wave surges, rushing through the gates, spreading their mantles, waving their olive branches, greeting, hailing, watching, and chatting.

What a change!

The emphasis seems to have shifted from the individual to the crowd, an observation that is confirmed by looking at the other panels presenting crowds: "The Way to Golgotha," "Pilate Washing His Hands," "The Scourging," "The Crowning with Thorns," "Christ before Herod," "Christ the Second Time before Pilate," and others. "It is not in the dramatic vividness of the posture and expression of individual figures, but in the silhouetting of the groups and their distribution in the panel, that Duccio's great imaginative power is felt," wrote Roger Fry.[3]

A token of the times, perhaps, for mankind was beginning to throw off the shackles of medieval thought. Man became an object to himself. And the liberation of the individual went hand in hand with the liberation of the masses. The people were clamoring for self-government and, toward the end of the thirteenth century, they were firmly entrenched in the government of the Commune of Siena.

Small wonder that this development should be reflected in the art of that great city at that particular time.

While impressed by the "people," the crowds, Duccio shows a tender veneration of woman; in which, perhaps, he is somewhat ahead of his time. For women, in the Commune of Siena, enjoyed little freedom, and little status—less than in other communes of the time.

Feminine tunics trail the floor; feminine *pallas* are pulled over the head, wrapping the whole body and leaving only the face free; maid servants' white headgear, colorful or gold-wrought shawls, begin to occupy strategic positions in Duccio's crowds: the center, the limelight.

Take his "Resurrection of Lazarus." The crowd pushes on under the craggy peaks and those trees, like two black accents; the crowd moves toward the opening of Lazarus' house of eternal rest, the coffin, standing upright, the lid just lifted. Lazarus is swathed in his shroud, with only his face free—an almost feminine figure. He is set off from the crowd, however, the one against the many. The crowd spreads in a downward movement, from left to right. At the center of this crowd—more central even than the space occupied by Jesus—is a woman looking up at him, over his outstretched hand. Her womanliness, in this crowd, is still more emphasized by the presence of another woman, kneeling in front of her to kiss the Savior's feet.

These wonderful faces of Duccio's women, incidentally, are all alike. It is really always the same woman: Madonna, angel, saint, or maidservant. The elongated, oval face, with its mel-

ancholy charm. The long, handsomely curved nose with the
swelling nostrils, the narrow lips, the rounded chin, and, above
all, the veiled look under lowered eyelids and gently curved
brows. Always the same face; whereas the masculine faces,
framed by beards or shaven, with long, flowing hair or short,
cropped locks, are far more individualized. This tendency to
stereotype women's faces while individualizing men's can be
traced in most primitives, and fits admirably into our whole
argument.*

Though women are present in Duccio's crowds, though these
crowds have a feminine dimension, it would be wrong to say
that his women dominate the crowd. And his crowd, after all,
still fails to fill a three-dimensional space. It remains a surface
group—still ornamental, in a Byzantine way.

When the crowd is really a crowd, we shall see how the subconscious of the artist time and again focuses on a female figure as though she were to symbolize, to *express,* the mass; as
though hers were the face we would obtain if, repeating the feat
of the experimental photographer, we were to mount all the
faces, distinguishable or indistinguishable, that make up that
crowd.

Hosts of men stampeding a plain; men in collective action;
men in frantic attack; men in rout: "The Battle of San Ro-
mano." Notice the captain, set off as an individual distinct from
the crowd that follows, characterized as a leader by his countenance, the whiteness of his horse, his advanced position. Then
turn your attention to the crowd. Helmets, visors, clanging
armor. Flags and halberds and motley trappings surge up from
the thronging dark of horses, corpses, orange trees. A mass in

---

* cf. the statement, by the eighteenth-century French philosopher, Mercier,
"La nature a semé beaucoup moins de variété dans le charactere des femmes
que dans celui des hommes. Presque toutes les femmes se ressemblent."
(*Songes et visions philosophiques,* Amsterdam, 1787)

motion. Only one head is bare; only one face is visible, accented
by the stormy illumination. It is a very young face, girlish, of
milk-white skin; a blond head of hair, with flowing curls. This
figure seems to symbolize the character of the mass—as seen
by Paolo Uccello—of which it is part.

"Fire in the Borgo." Human masses in panic, chased by the
flames and the wind, dragging out their aged and their infants,
from the left and the right to the foreground, up the stairs to
the Vatican Palace, where the motion ends, where the fire halts.

What is the face of this crowd?

Mothers and children occupy the whole foreground of the
painting, the women raising their rounded arms in prayerful
supplication while the wind plays in their abundant, flowing
hair and their loosely draped garments. Women busy themselves
to the right, hurry up the steps, cower in the back.

From the left, the men press in: pink-cheeked, beardless,
curly-haired, angel-faced. Only three virile types can be detected in the whole scene. One, enveloped in the darkness of
shadowy columns, is hardly visible. Another has stretched his
arms to receive a baby handed down to him by a mother from
the flaming ruins. His face is turned aside; some shadow seems
to fall on this one also, obscuring him, making him unrecog-
nizable. The third one is an old man resting on the shoulder of
a youth whose wavy mane covers up half of his face and expression. No doubt, the character of this crowd, as conceived
by Raphael, is definitely feminine.

How the doomsday crowds have swelled their ranks in the
course of the history of painting!

On primitive tablets and panels, you find two, three figures—
wise virgins or sheep—to enjoy the blessings of Paradise for
all of the saved; two, three figures—foolish virgins or rams—

to expiate in eternal hell-fire the sins of us all. Typically, the most important group in most early representations of the Last Judgment includes the Virgin Mary, standing or kneeling to the right of the Judge. For on this day of terror the prayers and the mediation of the mother should be more important than ever, the faithful seem to have thought.

Michelangelo's doomsday crowd is probably the most gigantic ever composed by the hand of an artist. To join this crowd in the Sistine Chapel causes almost incredible sensations. Huddled on the floor, the people of whom we are part, with their heads thrown back, their awed faces raised toward the ceiling, seem ready to soar with the blessed, or, shown to the door by the Judge's stern gesture, about to exit into the inferno that is this world of ours.

We look up and feel dwarfed; and to ask ourselves: is Michelangelo's crowd rather male or female in character seems a dwarfish question. Any question seems dwarfish, so colossal is this composition, so overwhelming, so crushing with the abundance of its detail.

But let us rebel, with the rebels fighting the angels up there. Look! These cohorts of angels rushing to the fore with the cross and the tokens of the passion, those angels raising the blessed and wrestling with the doomed—they have women's faces; there is no doubt about that.

The entire upper left section of the composition is dedicated to the blessed women: prominent among them, a mother caressing her child, and an Eve-like beauty running forward in innocent nakedness.

There is not much difference between the chaste, strong-featured, severe, yet ecstatic, faces of the blessed women, and the chaste, strong, yet immature, ecstatic faces of the blessed young men occupying the upper right section. The young men, the women, the angels: they are all sexless—slightly more feminine than masculine. Sexless, too, is all this exhibition of vig-

orous naked flesh, sexless as the nakedness of the masses of
flesh on a crowded beach. So similar, in fact, are men and
women, that the figure of St. John, among the blessed men,
has been mistaken for Eve by many scholars—as reported by
Redig da Campo in his monumental work on this Last Judgment.

As in the primitive representations, the Virgin Mother occupies her place to the Judge's right, enveloped in His glory.
Attired in dark red, with a sky-blue mantle on her knees, her
gentle face framed by a candid veil, her gaze is turned toward
the saved, soaring heavenward, as though she could not bear
the sight of those going down to everlasting despair.[4]

True, there are magnificent patriarchal figures in prominent
places: St. Peter, St. Bartholomew, St. Lawrence, St. Paul.
True, there are many things, infinitely many things. Yet is it
fanciful to say that the feminine element, in this gigantic crowd,
dominates more than the fifty per cent that would be its statistical due?

Look at Rubens' "little" "Judgment Day"!

Swarms of angels burst forth from angry heavens, and under their onrush, a formidable entanglement of human bodies,
as though squeezed from heaven in bunches. Down they drop,
their curvy bottoms, their rounded thighs and fleshy arms en-
twined, their naked torsos twisted in the most unlikely contor-
tions—especially those of the falling fallen women. Repeated,
over and again, the motif of woman—cause of damnation, center of damnation—dragged by her long hair by the seduced
Adam, down toward sinister, gaping depths, where the beautiful figures of women can be seen writhing in a lost fight against
the demons' grip.

Music, collective gaiety, twirls the peasants over the green
of the meadow, around the trees, dancing the "Wedding

Dance." Bruegel's stress on the communal element is so strong
that the aspect of the single faces becomes incidental. They all
look alike, well-nourished but sketchy, men's faces and wom-
en's. But if you step back from the canvas, half close your eyes
to perceive the whole, what you see is white blots : the kerchiefs
and aprons of these peasant women. They are swarming over
the whole expanse of this scene : white spots all over, like fes-
tive lampions losing themselves in a midsummer night's dream.
Reopening your eyes, you know that it is the brilliance of these
aprons and kerchiefs that rakes together the scattered, darker
figures of the men, joins them into this swarming, wheeling,
carousing collectivity. The decisive element of this crowd, too,
is feminine.

And where does Daumier end in his search for the character
of the crowd? Time and again his spotlight falls on a woman :
a flabby-breasted proletarian female protrudes from the huddle
of languishing bodies in his cartoon, "The Public Bath." She
seems to imbibe coolness for the whole crowd from the fresh
cascade that showers over her homely shoulders.

In the same way the dreariness of lower-class French life
finds its expression in a feminine group occupying the whole
first row of his "Third-Class Railway Carriage"—a mother
with babe in arms; an aged peasant woman folding tired hands
over a market-basket; a drowsing youngster, his head drooping
—not a virile head as yet—in the gloom of this carriage, where
the light from the small windows does not reach. Strong bones,
strong brows, tight lips; sorrowful and weary, yet endearing
and motherly : this is Daumier's woman. These are Daumier's
people.

Delacroix has his revolutionary crowd led by a woman—a
powerful woman, with naked breasts, in sweeping motion. A

rifle in one arm, the other raises the tricolor before the following mass. Liberty leading the people. Liberty? The will of this
people. The personification of this will. The Platonic idea of
the people. A woman.

We could go on. Think of the preponderance of leg-throw-
ing, or sumptuously dressed, watching, gossiping women in
Toulouse-Lautrec's "Moulin Rouge" series; think of the Bre-
ton white bonnets of the totally feminine crowd watching Gau-
guin's Jacob wrestling with the Angel, and all his flowery,
shiny-haired, flute-playing, naked, child-carrying, dancing, med-
itating groups of Tahitians. . . .

James Ensor is the crowd painter *par excellence*. His only
measure is delirium.

"Christ's Entry into Brussels" is simply wild. There is something Persian about this sea of colors.

Looking closer you note that the masculine faces in the foreground are dwarfed, distorted, or covered. The center foreground is occupied by two beaming ladies, one with whitish
blond curls, smartly dressed, with laughing eyes and a sensual
mouth; the other, in a Salvation Army bonnet, sagging cheeks,
an astonished little mouth, and raised eyebrows. The same pair
of rather striking ladies, incidentally, is met again in a much
later painting, "Ensor at the Harmonium," in a crowd that
shows many similarities with the Brussels crowd, except that
Ensor, the musician—now successfully established as a great
artist—is able to brave this crowd as an individual, while the
still struggling painter, back in 1899, depicted himself as Christ
within the crowd, tiny and quite overwhelmed, drowned by the
crowd.

Returning to the Brussels crowd: women are cramming in
from the right, three weird sisters in white collars and bonnets;

women swoon in the second row center, gaped at by more
women; women's faces dominate the left wing.

The soldiers are hats, hats, hats on blank faces; the only face
that sticks out among the foreshortened crowd in the rear, behind the struggling Savior, is a fat woman's.

Vive la Sociale is written on a standard waving over this in-
fernal apotheosis of a crowd.

The feminine character of the Ensor crowd comes out even
more strikingly in a study preceding the Brussels painting and
entitled "Hail Jesus, King of the Jews" (1885), where the
crowd consists altogether of women's faces. Three male figures, more particularized, more individuated, are separate to
the right, while the figure of the Savior is dissolved in light.

"Self-Portrait with Masks" (1899) is another version of the
same motif. He, Ensor, the individual, in and against a terrify-
ing crowd: the whole foreground is dominated by feminine
masks. And in "Old Woman and Masks," finally, the contrast
between individual and group seems to be obliterated, and the
naked expression, the hungry eyes, the mouth of withered sen-
suality, the wrinkles, the spots, the flowered hat, seem to stand
for, not *against* the crowd: to sum up, to symbolize its character.

> *Beguiling sex, without fear of god, withour honor*
>   *and without heart.*
> *Whirl of hypocrisies*
> *Crucible of lies and fakes*
> *Bogmire of malice*
> *Cave of rapine and of mortal sins*
> *Pandora's box*
> *Pond teaming with perverse beasts*
> *Slimy dungheap, wormy and drooling*
> *Surly marsh and hostile*
> *Horrible leech-infected sewer;*

Clawing beast with a snout of carnivorous canines
Lecherous bellows blowing hot and cold
Inspirer of the lowest beastliness
Betrayer of friends
Turkey-hen of seasoned flesh, haughty and foolish
Chicken-brained goose
Unscrupulous go-getter in search of accomplices
Weather-cock creaking to every vicious wind
Triple hole of perfidy, bottomless treachery, and
    devouring egotism
Full-bellied embodiment of a gigantic lie,
    gluttonously shaped by malicious gossip
Scourge of heaven and earth
Everlasting mask and endless smile.

This poem, as reported by Paul Haessaerts in his recent volume on James Ensor,[5] was written by Ensor in 1925 and entitled "About Women." It gives us a key, especially in the last line, to the understanding of the intuitively feminine character of Ensor's crowds: an explanation far more conclusive than our own analysis of his paintings. Ensor remains unsurpassed as a painter of the ferment, the agitation of the crowd, a theme that obsessed him. "Panicky configurations of human masses milling in senseless motion as though pushed on by malignant, mortal mass psychosis," says Werner Haftman. "Raw material of the human crowd, canaille that moans its anguish, wailing and lamenting."[6]

Ensor's crowds are masks and his masks are women, and his devastating judgment of woman reflects the deep crisis in the relationship between his ego, his individuality, and society, "the mass."

The most recent significant, epical representation of a crowd is Picasso's "Guernica." Overpowering, smashing, suggestive

of pain and contagious despair. But, in contrast to the great
crowds of past centuries, this crowd, like the "crowds" of the
ninth century, consists of six heads! That is all. But the light
still falls on the women; and women, rushing to the fore, hold-
ing the light, throwing up their arms, are the motion, the passion, the life and heart of this "crowd."

The painters of the second half of this century—exponents
of post-individual mankind—do not paint crowds any more. Go
to any exhibition, look at any book on contemporary painting,
to have the confirmation.

The primitive painter, the pre-individualist, we said, did not
see the crowd, did not paint the crowd. The crowd, as a topic
of painting, comes into existence as the artist advances in individuation, matures his individuality, and portrays triumphs,
battles, apocalypses, revolutions, hunting parties, with their
intuitively feminine traits. The crowd assumes oppressive, obses-
sive dimensions as the artist's relationship to society unbal-
ances. Small wonder that it disappears as an art topic, as his
individuality, like individuality in general, tends to disintegrate
and post-individual man takes the place of individual man.

It is interesting to note that women artists—barring exceptions—don't paint crowds. Not the few great women painters
who have made their way into the textbooks of art history, from
Angelica Kauffmann to Käthe Kollwitz, nor the many—an
ever-growing number—women painters of our day. The subject
somehow seems to be extraneous to the mind of the woman
painter, perhaps because it is too intimately intrinsic in the
deepest layers of her unconscious, so that she, like the primitive,
like the contemporary, fails to objectify it.

Speaking of women painters, we cannot help admitting that
their production in the course of art history is thin, surprisingly
thin. While there are numbers of really great poetesses—from

Sappho to Gabriela Mistral—novelists, and scientists, the women painters worth remembering can be counted on the fingers of one hand; and there are no women composers to speak of.

Much has been speculated as to the reason for the relative failure of women in these fields. Women are less imaginative, it has been claimed. Women are less creative, all their creativity having been channeled by providence into the production of children. This, of course, is pure nonsense and does not stand up in the face of modern psychological research. If women were not imaginative, not creative enough to paint and compose, they could not create poetry; they could not create great fiction, either. Art is art.

The reason would seem to lie elsewhere.

It is a fact that talent in the figurative arts and in music "runs in the family," much more so than poetry or fiction writing: the son of a painter very often shows talent for painting, too. And an amazingly high percentage of composers are the sons of composers—Mozart! Bach!—or, at any rate, of musicians.

Why? There is no evidence that musical talent, or pictorial talent, is more inheritable than literary talent. And yet . . .

Perhaps the explanation is that painting and music are formidable powers in conditioning the environment. A child exposed during his formative years from morning to evening to the sound of music, as happens in a musician's home, will absorb it, will imbibe it, willy-nilly. A toddler playing in the studio of his painter father or mother, messing with colors while other children are playing with dolls or electric trains, will naturally grow into the world of art. Assuming that the percentage of talented children is the same in artistic as in nonartistic families—inasmuch as "artistic genes" simply do not exist—the environment is bound to work as a selective factor, bringing out more talent in artistic families than in others.

Literature is different. It is not absorbed directly, through the senses, unconsciously, pre-consciously. The young person applies himself to it usually at a later age than the color-dabbling or piano-pounding toddler, in a solitary corner of the house, to clarify his mind on issues he dares not discuss with anyone, perhaps, or to relieve his secret passions and anxieties. Although table conversations, family interests undoubtedly have *something* to do with it, the young person's approach to poetry and fiction is far more individual, personal, than to painting and music, which are, as it were, irresistibly imposed by the environment.

Now, if this environment is patriarchal and does not take girls' endeavors as seriously as boys', and is adverse to women's independent affirmation, it will be more inhibitive in the more environment-bound fields of painting and music than in the relatively personal sphere of literature. Hence, many a poetess, many a woman novelist has been able to nurture and mature a great work in the silence of an isolated village home (as Grazia Deledda), or in her room in the attic (as Charlotte Brontë), or in the intervals between domestic chores (as Jane Austen), while women painters have been rare, and women composers, practically speaking, are missing from the history of music—music being the most invading, group-conditioning and group-conditioned of all the art media.

This is true for, let us say, the last two thousand years of our civilization. It is true of civilized—nowadays, all patriarchal —societies.

Sophie Drinker points out that it has not always been so. Music and magic, she says, documenting most meticulously, were originally woman's domain.[7]

Women, in primitive societies, "sang"—that is, composed and executed the music—for the safe return of their menfolk from hunting and war parties. They "sang" their babes into life and accompanied, with their own dirges, the dead into the happy hunting grounds. Thus, religious music, Mrs. Drinker claims, was probably first made by women. Also, "the form of the work song probably originated with women. . . . Such a development of musical imagination may be assumed from the fact that women are believed to have worked in groups long before men organized themselves for pursuits other than hunting and fighting—neither of which adapts itself to rhythmic action."

Painting, too, was originally magic. According to Mrs. Drinker, ". . . the recognized authority of women in matters of birth and rebirth indicates strongly that designing and painting were also an evidence of women's magic powers, and that many of the rock paintings were women's work. . . . Only the erroneous notion of many nineteenth-century scholars that women do not function imaginatively has established the fiction that the pictures were all the work of men artists."

With the emergence of individualistic society, magic is broken, and creativity in artistic expression dies down in women. For "loss of leadership, or lack of a chance to lead, is a barrier to creative work that ranks second to none."

This loss, however, being socially conditioned, is not irreparable; and with the emancipation of women in post-individual society, we are witnessing, indeed, a return of an ever-growing number of women to the ranks of creative artists: painters, first; composers, second. If really first-rate results are still lacking—at least as far as music is concerned—this is because post-individual society is as yet in its infancy.

Mrs. Drinker does not suggest that women apply themselves to the writing of great symphonies in the nineteenth-century style, or to any form of "detached" music such as characterized the individualist era. She recommends that women take the initiative in bringing about a new social integration of music: music as healer, in sickrooms and mental hospitals; music as pacifier in areas of social or racial tension; music, in other words, as a new "magic"—Orphic music—but on a conscious level. Sounds and forms unheard of may be created in this music of the future. According to Mrs. Drinker, women have already done some pioneering work in this direction.

An analogous argument could, of course, be made for painting, and its development away from the virtuosities of the Great Masters and toward some form of social integration. A reintegration of painting with architecture, and industrial design with life is possible—a return to "magic": Orphic painting, in the form of art-therapy; the healing use of stimulating or soothing color in mental hospitals, even in the homes for the blind, who, though unable to perceive colors through the eye, yet are pervaded, through the skin, as it were, by the intensity and rhythm of colors.

"Women," Rimbaud prophesied, "will find the unknown. Will her ideational worlds be different from ours? She will come upon strange, unfathomable, repellent, delightful things. We shall take them; we shall comprehend them."

This trend toward the social integration of art follows, or goes hand in hand with, a trend toward individual disintegration—the disintegration of the artist's objective reality, the annulment of the distance between subject and object, content and form, intention and expression, artist and society, I and other.

But this, precisely, is the realm of magic. This is "primitive." For what is magic but this identification, this placing of my will and your reality on the same level, so that the former is able to act on the latter? It is the identification of inside and outside, of nature and man, of spirit and matter, of group action and individual destiny.

Thus, the return of post-individual art to the primitivism of pre-individual art is not a fad, but corresponds to a deep and

pervasive psychological reality. And it goes amazingly far—
farther than most contemporary artists are aware.

I have before me a charcoal drawing by Picasso, entitled
"The Violin" (1912), and, next to it, "Goddess of Fertility,"
from Cyprus, *c.* 2500–2000 B.C., reproduced in Erich Neumann's *The Great Mother*.[8] Picasso most certainly did not know
this image, but the similarity is amazing. The frequent appearance of stringed instruments in still lifes—Braque, Matisse, Picasso, Juan Gris, Chagall—is in itself interesting, as they seem
to go back to certain female figurines, found in the Cyclades
and dated 2500 B.C. These look exactly like cellos or violas da
gamba.

Next to stringed instruments, the bottle is probably the one
object that dies hardest in non-objective still lifes. Take Le
Corbusier's still life of 1920, or the innumerable variations on
that theme in Morandi's paintings and drawings. Prehistoric
art, on the other hand, is full of bottle-vessel-women, whose
symbolism has been beautifully elucidated by Erich Neumann.

Yet there are differences between pre-individual and post-
individual art: between the art of the primitives and our own.

I asked a great sculptor recently: "Where is the difference?
Can you put your finger on it? The difference between your
horses and riders and the horses and riders of the pre-individual
matriarchal Etruscans?"

"The difference," he answered, "is in the artists' temperaments. What came spontaneously among the primitives, is lu-
cubrated in contemporary art. The contemporary artist is too
cerebral; he is more of an intellectual than the primitive. Therefore his work lacks the magic power of the primitive."

Then I asked another one, an Italian sculptor who has peopled a world of his own with magic monsters and totems. "I
see no difference at all," he replied. "We look for the essential,

and what is essential is eternal. Therefore, we see things the same way the primitives did."

Then he added: "Of course, we admire the mastery, the virtuosity, the elegance, the *knowledge* of the great artists of classical Greece, of the Renaissance, but we have seen this art go to pieces, this virtuosity become ever more exterior, this elegance become vain exhibitionism. I was in Greece, and I assure you the archaic sculpture of Mycenae today speaks more directly to us, is more 'true' in its simplicity, than the most labored statue of Phidias. To forget oneself in nonbeing is what pre-individual and post-individual artists have in common."

These two testimonies do not contradict each other; they are complementary. The artists' "temperaments" are different. That is, where in pre-individual art there was a simple acceptance of the unitary magic cosmos of which we are part, post-individual art is based on a good deal of conscious, intellectual rejection of what has come later, on a return to origins. Pre-individual art, we might say, is tradition-directed: a resultant of the group-force time-vector. Post-individual art is other-directed: a resultant of the group-force space-vector. This also means that pre-individual art is bound to a locale, whereas post-individual art is universal.

But both are genuine expressions of a strikingly similar, even though not identical, psychological situation: a "collectivism," with the "group-force" tending to integrate individual and group, inside and outside, I and other, man and nature, energy and matter, science and art. This has been in the past, and is now, the climate in which the feminine can thrive.

Therefore this resurgence of feminine symbolism in art; therefore this new participation of women in creative art, unprecedented in historic times. Not the art of the "great man," a nineteenth-century leftover, that is rapidly disappearing from the stage of world history, but an art that expresses the reality of our age with means that need not shrink from the technical and scientific conquests of the past millennium. In such an art, men and women will share alike.

As in the preceding chapters, our attack has been two-pronged : the collective and the feminine as expressed in paintings ; and the collective and the feminine in painting, that is, in the history of painting.

We have seen, indeed, that the more real a crowd is in a painting, the more it is permeated by feminine elements. In making this assertion, however, we do not wish to exaggerate. Looking for the expression of the artist's subconscious associations in a painting is like looking for shapes in clouds or in a Rorschach blot. Everyone is free to see, more or less, what he wishes to see ; and what one sees is often more revealing of the psychology of the observer than of him who made the painting.

With this caveat, we should like to ask the reader to look at the paintings here discussed, or at others, and decide for himself whether he sees what we see.

As for the association of the collective and the feminine in the history of painting, it seems to us the only valid explanation for women's past apparent inferiority in painting, as well as in music. The inferior position in which women find themselves in patriarchal societies inhibits artistic creativity and works as a selective factor in favor of male supremacy. The male artist is privileged by the "social genes," even though, individually, there is no genetic difference at all between male and female artists. In pre-individual society, women are as proficient as men, or more so, in art and music, which is collective expression, which is magic, which is great art. The ever-accelerating evolution of our society toward new forms of collectivism is setting the feminine element in new relief, is restimulating feminine talent. We have a chance now. Let us wait and see the results.

SIX

Women in Neverland

A map of the world that does not include Utopia is not worth even glancing at.

OSCAR WILDE[1]

Ever since Adam ate of the Tree of Knowledge and became aware of his individuality as set apart from the collective—Eve: "The Church"—there have been problems, problems. And as long as there have been problems, man has dreamed of solving them: projecting the solution into a golden past or a rosy future, here or beyond, onto faraway islands or nowhere; the whereabouts of his projection has depended upon whether he has been a pessimist or an optimist, a romantic or a rationalist, an idealist or a materialist. You can divide the Utopians along any of these lines.

We are going to look at them from a different angle.

Let us take, on the one hand, those thinkers who, in planning for the happiness of the human race, begin with the organization as a whole, on the theory that when the perfection of the collective is assured, the individual will be all right—if he stays in his right place.

At the other end, there are those who take society for granted. Everybody has either his penthouse, his tail-finned car, and his ever-pouring bar, as in a Hollywood movie—even though no one knows where it all comes from—or he has his ennobling poverty. Everybody has the background, the setting in which he can perfect his individuality, if you only leave him alone. When all individuals are perfect, society will be perfect.

The first group of thinkers—considering only our own Western tradition—begins, let us say, with Plato and ends with Lenin. The second goes back to Aristotle's critique of Plato and finds its most rabid expression in Nietzsche.

Between the two extremes we find a wide range of thinkers drawing, in various proportions, elements from both ends. In the middle, with Jean Jacques Rousseau, individualism and collectivism are theoretically in perfect equilibrium. For what Rousseau proposes is "to find a form of association which may defend and protect with the whole force of the community the person and property of every associate, and by means of which, coalescing with all, he may nevertheless obey only himself, and remain as free as before." (That, practically, Rousseau leans much more heavily toward the side of individualism, we shall discuss later.)

As one would expect, women fare exceedingly well in the collectivist Utopias, where they are liberated and exalted; whereas they get a rough deal, occupying a lowly place, in the individualists' paradise.

This is so obvious that we need not spill much ink over it. For the collectivist, or socialist, in the real sense of the word, is, and has always been, in favor of the underdog; since woman is an underdog, he is in favor of woman.

Obvious though this reasoning may seem, it is not convincing. Plato, for example, did not propose the liberation of the slaves. Yet he proposed the liberation of women. The reason, therefore, must lie elsewhere.

Woman and slave, or underdog, or chattel, are connected in either of two ways, in economic history. Either woman is the prototype of property, and her fall from an originally superior position to that of a possession of a patriarchal husband marks the beginning of private property in general. Or the institution of private property, due to the accumulation of possessions in the hands of an individual male, entailed male dominance in general, and therefore dominance over women. The former position was held by Thorstein Veblen; the latter, by Engels and the Marxists.

In either case, the first cause remains shrouded in darkness. If we accept Veblen's thesis, we should ask ourselves why woman should have fallen from her originally higher position. Did her biological condition undergo a sudden change? And in the Marxian hypothesis : why did property accumulate in the hands of the male rather than those of the female?

The most plausible explanation comes from W. I. Thomas in his now classic *Sex and Society*. He seems to side with Engels rather than with Veblen. While "on account of the more stationary condition of woman and the greater mobility of men" the earliest groupings of population were about women rather than men, a revolution occurred, displacing women from the pivot of society, when men introduced their hunting and warring experience, the fashioning of weapons, the use of animals, into agriculture and industry and thus displaced and subjugated women. The final subjugation of women thus is not due to superior muscular strength, but to a "more widely developed technique of production, and to the wealth produced thereby."[2]

Whichever the cause and whichever the effect, it is generally assumed that the rise of private property and the subjugation of woman are related phenomena, and that, therefore, any solution of problems created by the former and its corollaries is inseparable from a solution of the problems entailed by the latter.

The more radical the socialism of a planner, the more organic will be the structure of his ideal society; and this organism does not tolerate the growth of sub-organisms imposing their own laws on the prime cell or atom of society, which is the individual. Among the sub-organisms that cannot be tolerated is the closed patriarchal family. No matter what the avowed purpose of a totalitarian-collectivist order, it tends to undermine the family. This can be seen in communist societies just as under Nazism and Fascism, and even in free but other-directed societies such as our own.

But in coming to grips with the patriarchal family, the planners of a collective order had to tackle the problem of the relations between men and women—to equalize the bricks with which to build the social structure.

Since earliest times, social planners of the collectivist type have looked to the social insects as an ideal form of organization. Plutarch, for example, describes the reforms of the Spartan Lycurgus in the following terms: "In short, Lycurgus habituated his countrymen to forego private life, even to forget how to live it. Just like bees, they always identified themselves with the commonwealth, swarming about their king, and devoted body and soul to the service of their country."

That the "king of the bees" is really a queen was not known in antiquity; and that "to forego private life, even to forget how to live it" implied the emancipation of women, was not known, but intuited, by the Greeks—by the Spartans in practice, by Plato in theory, as we shall see forthwith.

The bee stage of collectivization, however, has never been reached by human society. The biological reasons for this, as scientists today know, are the family as we know it, and the relations between men and women, as we know them. "First let us remind ourselves," says Julian Huxley, "that . . . we with our human type of society must give up any hope of developing such altruistic instincts as those of the social insects. It would be more correct to say that this is impossible so long as our species continues its present reproductive habits."[3] If, like the social insects, we were to specialize reproduction—by adopting the system advocated by geneticists like Muller or Brewer and caricatured in Aldous Huxley's *Brave New World*—and if we were to emancipate women as workers and the pivot of the social organism, then, and only then, could we humans achieve a state of total socialization.

These are the historic, economic, social, and biological reasons for which all socialists or collectivists have advocated, and are advocating, the emancipation of woman, her full equality with men. Reasons—or perhaps, rationalizations—of the deep, underlying, all-pervasive fact of the affinity between the collective and the feminine.

In the following pages we shall take a look at the position of women in some of the most characteristic collectivist Utopias, and, for contrast, in more or less individualist blueprints.

Plato's Republic is a timocracy, which means, the rule of honor. The rule is not that of the best men, which would be aristocracy, but the rule of a principle, *timos,* embodied in the guardians of the State, who—amazing to imagine at that time! —are both men and women.

But let us enter the State in the company of Philosopher Kings and see for ourselves.

It is night, the poet sings, night in the glade, in the rocky cave. Full shines the moon when the women, harmoniously, on light feet, begin to circle the altar on the soft, new-risen grass.

The sacrifices are ready. Blood is flowing. There is wood-smoked aroma of freshly broiled slices of meats. There is honey. There are loaves—the gifts of Persephone—and there is wine.

> *Eros, I sing, the languid,*
> *Decked with flower-heavy garlands,*
> *Eros, lord of mankind*
> *And master of the gods.*

Thus sings the poet in Doric or Phrygian strains—the strains of necessity and the strains of freedom.

"They are the only modes the government will let us use," the poet whispers into our ear during an interval. "All other modes are banned. And no innovation is authorized. We must do our utmost to keep these forms and modes intact; for any musical innovation is full of danger to the whole State and ought to be prohibited. When the modes of music change, the fundamental laws of the State always change with them."[4]

From far, far away, we can discern Stalin, Lenin and Khrushchev nodding approval.

"Stability," the World Controller says. "The world is stable now. People are happy: they get what they want, and they never want what they can't get. . . . Ours is the stablest equilibrium in history," he adds. "China's was hopelessly insecure by comparison; even the primitive matriarchies weren't steadier than we are. . . ."[5]

> *Eros, like a lumberjack,*
> *Cut me down with a mighty axe*
> *And pitched me adrift*
> *Into the torrent of winter.*

We wonder about the extraordinary beauty of the youths and maidens who dance, naked, around the altars. The harmony of proportions, the measure of movements. The vigor, the nimbleness.

"They are Alphas," the Director of the Hatcheries explains.

"God has mixed gold in the composition of these," the poet says. "They are the guardians. Others he has made of silver, to be auxiliaries."

"The Betas," corrects the Director of the Hatcheries.

"Others, again, who are to be husbandmen and craftsmen, he has composed of brass and iron."

"The Deltas and Epsilons."

By that time the fires have died down, the music, hinting at a few relaxed Ionian strains, soft drinking harmonies, has been hushed, and the divine-looking young people, have disappeared in groups of two and three in the surrounding rock caves and wood thickets.

Childbirth was so easy at that time. Maybe the gods looked on more benevolently, or the midwives' magic worked more efficiently, or it was just earlier in the calendar of evolution.

But these women did not fuss. They went about their business, hunting, warring, and administering the State, and when the hour came, they lay down, by the river, under the willow, in a cave, in the olive grove, and delivered the child, and carried it home, where appropriate officers would be waiting—men and women, indiscriminately—to examine the new arrival. If his quality turned out to be below the "gold" standard, they would dispose of him; but if he was found good, they would take him to the "fold," to be raised there. The women went on minding their own business, hunting, warring, and administering the State.

If, as these "Republicans" tell us, the difference between women and men "consists only in women bearing and men begetting children," and if the bearing of children and bringing them into this world is such an incidental and easy matter, then, indeed, the difference between the sexes is incidental and of no consequence, and it is logical that they should have the same education, the same pursuits, the same offices. "There is nothing peculiar in the constitution of women," Plato said, "which would affect them in the administration of the State."

The differences between the sexes he compared to the difference in nature between bald men and hairy men:

> . . . then, if bald men are cobblers, should we forbid the hairy men to be cobblers, and conversely? . . . We never meant, when we constructed the State, that the opposition of natures should extend to every difference, but only to those differences which affected the pursuit in which the individual is engaged. . . . And if, I said, the male and female sex appear to differ in their fitness for any art or pursuit, we should say that such pursuit or art ought to be assigned to one or the other of them; but if the difference consists only in women bearing and men begetting children, this does not amount

to a proof that a woman differs from a man in respect to the sort of education she should receive; and we shall therefore continue to maintain that our guardians and their wives ought to have the same pursuits.

When they were full of milk—and they were, for they were strong women and healthy, golden women, and it was early in the calendar of evolution—they went to the "fold." Provided, that is, the nursing did not interfere with their work or with their rest. The law provided plenty of wet nurses for this contingency. But when they went to the fold, they played and laughed with all the little animals, and suckled them. They did not know the one they had given birth to from the others, nor did they care. They were all golden babies, and each belonged to all, and all to each. "People are happy," the World Controller said. "They're plagued with no mothers or fathers. . . ."

So they were raised in the fold, the children's house, boys and girls together. They were trained in gymnastics, wrestling naked in the arena. Gymnastics, Plato said, made the girls resemble boys. And they were trained in music, which made the boys resemble girls. He knew that as well as the twentieth-century sociologists.

They were given swift but gentle horses, to follow their "parents"—all the older generation were their parents—to battle; and there they became inured to death, which they did not dread—they were "death-conditioned"—and to seeing heroes and heroines fighting bravely. And when the battle was over, the valiant women were honored and celebrated no less than the valiant men; the fallen were buried with all the pomp befitting heroes; but those who survived had the right to choose a youth or girl of their liking, and kiss him, or her; nor did the chosen one have a right to refuse the kiss.

And then they went to the big house of the Guardians and Auxiliaries, where everything was held in common, and there was no piece of property, no instant of privacy. "People are never alone now," the World Controller said. "We make them hate solitude, and we arrange their lives so that it's almost impossible for them ever to have it."

And then it was night, night in the glade and the rocky cave. Full shone the moon when close to the altar they paused.

For the Guardians had counted the young in the fold and the number was found wanting. And the Guardians know the number, representing a geometrical figure, which has control over the good and evil of birth and will assure a just crop of golden babies and maintain the stability of the State.

Thus, they united the maidens, who had been crowned with victory in battle, and let them choose among the best of the Guardians and Auxiliaries.

> *Hymen, Hymen. Of*
> *Eros I sing, the languid,*
> *Decked with flower-heavy garlands.*
> *Eros, lord of mankind*
> *And master of the gods.*

The Brave New World is a nightmare; the Republic, a dream. The realities from which they take off are diametrically opposed. Huxley's is a world of Science; Plato's is pre-scientific. Plato heralds the dawn of the individual; Huxley witnesses his dusk. And yet the similarities between the structures of the two imaginations are striking.

Stability is a key word for both. Collective justice determines individual justice, and the State is planned for the happiness of all, not for the individual, who can draw his personal happiness only from the collective one. Stability and individuality, indeed, are at loggerheads. While Plato hopes for the perfection of his individual within his perfect State, his hope is bound to remain frustrated. What the pre-individualist Plato only intuits, the post-individualist Huxley knows; and gleefully he dissolves the human face, the human identity, in a thousand identical faces of groups of "Bokanovsky twins."

The women in the Brave New World, of course, are not plagued by feminine drudgeries and problems any more than are the women in the Republic. They are bred in all castes. Those we have occasion to meet personally, the Alpha-Pluses, are independent, in responsible positions, quite on a par with the men. The family is dissolved, the sexual hierarchy abolished. Sex no longer is caste. Yet, there must be something intrinsically inferior in the women of the Brave New World, for the big shots—the World Controllers, the Directors of the Hatcheries, the Chief Community Songsters—are all men.

This, it seems to me, is a mistake in the conception. Total de-individualization should have entailed gynecocracy. Or maybe we are still early in the era of Our Ford. The changes wrought by this civilization are, above all, technical. The effects on the socio-psychological level have not yet matured. For the people in the Brave New World, and their relations with one another, are still gruesomely similar to the people of our own world—including the women—and their relations. Maybe, when Mr. Huxley goes to visit his Brave New World next time, he'll find it administered by mighty, dreadful women of a special caste. The logic of things would postulate it.

On Plato—the Pythagorean, the metamathematician—the law of collective-feminine affinities worked more powerfully. The step he had to take, moreover, from the dreary, psychologically starved and locked-up Athenian matron—as we know her, especially, from the comedies—to the free, heroic warrior woman, the philosopher-queen-guardian-woman of his Republic, was much longer, indeed, than the step Huxley had to take from the emancipated, active women of his own society to the emancipated, active women of his Brave New World. What Huxley took for granted, and therefore did not push any further, Plato had to discover for himself. He had to tackle the problem as if it were a giant tree, and pull it up by its roots.

And indeed he did. In addition to sporadic references throughout the work, Book V of *The Republic* is entirely dedicated to the woman question: to rationalizing, to externalizing the inner logic of its structure. It gives many good reasons for the basic fact that a collective order—in the sense in which Plato's Republic is collectivist—necessarily implies the end of the family as we know it, the end of sex as caste, the emancipation of women and their equalization with men. For this is the physical-mathematical action of group-force on sex balance.

Plato knew what he was in for. He knew he was going to be made fun of. He anticipated the satire of the reactionary, aristocratic Aristophanes, whose perfect American club women, become rulers of the State, are still very funny today. And the criticism of the more individualistic Aristotle, who derides his communism as "fallacious . . . impracticable . . . a source of weakness," and warns of giving women too much power and liberty, which always gives bad results, as could be seen in Sparta.

"As we have determined to speak our minds," brave new Plato says, "we must not fear the jests of the wits which will be directed against this sort of innovation; how they will talk of women's attaintments both in music and gymnastics, and above all about their wearing armor and riding upon horseback!" And then: "Having begun, we must go forward to the rough places of the law."

There was no way out—so cogent was the logic of the matter.

Cicero was a conservative. He thought little of the people. He was frightened by the masses. Woe, if the mob is aroused. ". . . Under such conditions, even the slaves come to behave with unseemly freedom. Wives have the same rights as husbands, and in the abundance of liberty, even the dogs, the horses, and the asses are so free in their running about, that men must make way for them in the street."[6]

As we see, Cicero thought little of women, too. Husbands and fathers had to have absolute jurisdiction over them in *his* Republic. Their only virtues were chastity, modesty, and obedience. If the masses, or the women, get out of hand, the State is in for evil days.

The Utopian communism of Sir Thomas More is tempered by a millennium of Christianity, by his personal, strong individualism, by his experience as a statesman whose *Realpolitik* was far from communist principles or ideas of religious tolerance. The man who resigned his high office over the issue of the king's divorce could not advocate the community of women in his ideal state. The community of More's Utopia,[7] in fact, is based on a patriarchal order, where "wives obey their husbands and the young obey the old."

This is a broad declaration of traditional principles. Let us see how far the Utopians really live up to them, or are able to live up to them.

Let us meet the subjects of Utopia, men and women. They are dressed alike, "covered homely with leather or skins that will last seven years; and when they go forth they cast upon them a cloak which hideth the other homely apparel. These cloaks throughout the whole island be all of one color, and that is the natural color of the wool."

Although born each into his individual household, to his individual mother, the Utopian babies are raised together in communal nurseries, in great public buildings, tended in common by mothers and wet nurses. And although the family, evidently, is based on mutual affection, there is something strangely statistical attached to these Utopian children: for, if there are too many in one family, the excess is transferred to another, where there are too few; in another town; even, if necessary, in another continent. Thus the family, in spite of its religious foundation, ceases to be a biological unit.

All Utopian children, boys and girls, receive the same education. Until the age of five, they stay in the nursery, after which age, and until they get married, they serve at the tables of the common halls, where the whole community enjoys its nourishing and most pleasurable meals. "For it were a folly to take the pain to dress a bad dinner at home, when they may be welcome to good and fine fare so nigh hand at the hall." The women of every family, by turn, have the office and charge of cookery, "for seething and dressing the meat, and ordering of all things thereto belonging." Thereto belonging includes music at every dinner, the burning of perfumes and fine herbs, and anything that might make the common meal more pleasurable.

Thus the drudgery of the private household is abolished. Communalized are child care, cooking, and also the nursing of the sick, for whom the community has provided splendid hospitals.

The women, in fact, have no time to waste on chores that are more rationally taken care of by the community. For two years they must join, together with the men, in the labor draft, in charge of the nation's agriculture. For "husbandry is a science in common to all in general, both men and women, wherein they be all expert and cunning." Out in the country, on splendidly equipped, State-owned farms, these men and women learn to sow and reap and raise cattle. They also bring up "a great multitude of poultry, and that by a marvellous policy. For the hens do not sit upon the eggs, but by keeping them in a certain equal heat they bring life into them, and hatch them." Thus, the Utopians had invented the incubator, a good half-millennium before its time! They also were far advanced in animal psychology and knew about "imprinting" chick brains. For, we are told, "the chickens, as soon as they come out of the shell, follow men and women instead of hens," just like Professor Konrad Lorenz's trains of "imprinted" ducklings. It is only to be hoped that More's foresight in matters of social organization was as clear as in matters touching upon husbandry and animal psychology.

To return now to the Utopian women: once out of the labor draft, each one learns a craft, just as the men do, for the State needs smiths and carpenters and masons and weavers and spinners. And "of the aforesaid crafts every man learneth one. And not only the men, but also the women. But the women, as the weaker sort, be put to the easier crafts, as to work wool and flax. The more laborsome sciences be committed to men." But no "science" is really too laborsome. The working day has been reduced to six hours, three before lunch, and three in the afternoon. The rest of the day is given over to studies, the cultivation of the pleasures of the mind. The working day usually starts with a lecture on some subject of general interest, either on philosophy or on literature or music or science; these lectures are attended by both men and women.

Thus there are no household chores. Property is held neither by men nor by women. And education, adult education, and work are common to both.

As to domestic relations—as far as they exist—marriage is entered on a basis of complete equality, preceded by the much-cited mutual "inspection." A respectable matron presents the bride-to-be naked to her future husband; a respected older man presents the groom-to-be naked to the future wife. Although we are told, on one occasion, that "the husbands chastise their wives, and the parents their children," the rights of both husband and wife, as spelled out, seem to be exactly the same. Adultery is punished equally, whether committed by man or woman; and divorce, and the right to remarry, is granted to the guiltless party, whether man or woman, whereas the guilty party, whether man or woman, has to live a life of celibacy and infamy. Divorce is also granted in cases of mutual incompatibility, but not before the court has tried everything possible to reconcile the parties. If a marriage ends in divorce by mutual consent, both parties are free to remarry.

In public life we see that the "aldermen," or "philarchs," elected by every fifty families, and the "tranibores" elected by every ten philarchs, and the prince, elected by the assembly of all two hundred existing tranibores, are all men. This seems to be in contradiction with the real structure of the society. We wonder whether the narrator, Raphael the sailor, did not simply forget to mention that there were women among these rulers. The more so since the priesthood, which is elective like the office of philarch and tranibore, and is really the highest and most honored in the whole community, is open to women, as mentioned in passing by the narrator. "The priests, unless they be women (for that kind is not excluded from priesthood, howbeit few be chosen, and none but widows and old women), the men priests, I say, take to their wives the chiefest women in all their country. For to no office among the Utopians is more honor and pre-eminence given. In so much that if they commit any offence they be under no common judgment but be left only to God and themselves."

Thus we feel tempted to ascribe these traces of patriarchism in Utopia, which can be detected in a few broad generic assertions rather than in detailed descriptions of the circumstances, to some distortion in the eye of the narrator-author, reared and conditioned as he was in a strictly patriarchal environment, rather than to the inner logic of the communist-collective structure of the State, which implies the emancipation of women and their equalization with men.

The inhabitants of Bacon's New Atlantis[8] have gone through no revolution. Miraculously inspired by the purest sort of Christian faith, they are not anxious to change existing institutions, but rather to perfect themselves individually within the traditional framework. As individuals, they seem to be freer, more independent of control by the State than More's Utopians. Undoubtedly, Bacon has a far greater respect for the individual, for the fullness and elegance of human personality, than does More. Life in New Atlantis seems far less socialized. It takes place in rich and happy private homes. There is no trace of communism.

Poor women, therefore: prolific mothers and honored housewives, whose only privilege is to serve their husbands. Some menial, subordinate work is conceded to them. We see them at the House of Solomon, that magnificent national academy of arts and sciences, at the last minute, just before taking leave of Atlantis. "We have also, as you must think, novices and apprentices, that the succession of the former employed men do not fail; besides a great number of servants and attendants, men and women."

And it is logical that this should be so.

The soldier-women, clad and armed like men, who meet the stranger before the gates of Campanella's City of the Sun,[9] are reincarnations of the Platonic women. Muscular and agile, tall and tanned, they present a picture of natural beauty. Artificial embellishments, like make-up or high heels, apt to conceal aesthetic flaws that are the outer signs of moral flaws, are punished with death. Born free into this free and happy society that knows neither slaves nor servants, the Solar girls receive the same education as the boys, with a curriculum providing a careful balance between intellectual work, manual labor, and sport. They are qualified for the same jobs and duties, manual, mechanical, or intellectual, the only difference being that those tasks requiring physical effort or long marches—such as plowing, sowing, harvesting—are performed by the males, whereas the women take care of milking the cows, preparing the cheeses, and working the nearby orchards. Women are exempted from work with iron or wood. If a woman shows an aptitude for painting, she may ply this art. Music, on the other hand, is a field altogether reserved to women, which is without precedent in history or fiction; it is unlikely that Campanella knew about woman's role in the musical life of the primitives.

The women also prepare the food and set the common table, but the serving at table is entrusted to boys and girls under twenty years of age.

Women, furthermore, are in charge of preparing medicines and drugs which, inasmuch as this is a "stationary" art not requiring either physical effort or long marches, is particularly suitable to their nature.

Plato had noted that strong-minded but weak-bodied persons make the most skillful physicians; in his Republic, women would fall into this category. In the Republic, however, medicine does not occupy nearly so important a place as it does in the City of the Sun, where the cures for the most important sicknesses are, so to speak, written into the Constitution. The task assigned to women in medicine, which is magic, in this communist Utopia is particularly interesting in view of the role they played as physicians in pre-individual society, and are beginning to play again in post-individual, especially in communist, societies, to which we shall return in Chapter IX.[10]

Beautiful women, strong women, active women, free women. Not tied by any bonds of family; for the family is totally abolished. Not subject to paternal or other masculine tutelage or authority. A free-moving atom in this society, dependent only— and on an equal footing with man—on its laws and their enactment by the all-powerful organs of the State.

Women, together with men, participate in the Great Assembly

that elects the Highest Authorities: Hoh, the chief executive, with his three under-secretaries, Pon (Power), Sin (Sapience), and Mor (Love). These, however, all happen to be men. I say "happen to be" because we are not told anywhere that women are excluded from the higest office. Sin, at least, who adminis- ters the sciences, or Mor, who presides over matters of social organization and regulates procreation and the evolution of the species, really should be women.

But here, it would seem, Campanella's imagination, like More's, balks. A woman occupying the higest office of the ideal State—that is an idea that would not enter his mind. He did not even deem it necessary to exclude the possibility.

We say "of the ideal State," for Campanella was fully aware of the power of women in the real States of his time. According to him, astrological constellations favored a "government of women in this century."

The proof of it is that the government of women has prevailed in our time. New Amazons have appeared between Nubia and Monopotama, and in Europe we have seen the reign of Rossalene in the Ottoman Empire, Bona in Poland, Mary in Hungary, Elizabeth in England, Catherine in France, Bianca in Tuscany, Marguerite in Belgium, Mary in Scotland, Isabella, who sponsored the dis- covery of the New World, in Spain. . . . The constellations have favored the discovery of new empires, the possibility of circum- navigating the world, and the government of women.

At a closer examination, Campanella's "communism," though prescribing the absolute abolition of private property, the com- munity of homes, beds, and tables, the equality of dress for all, is limited—as can be seen even more clearly from a reading of his *Political Aphorisms*,[11] which preceded the *City of the Sun* by a few years. On more than one occasion he warns here against the incompetence of the masses to rule themselves, or even to elect the best possible ruler if granted universal suffrage—and this in terms that so clearly characterize him as an aristocrat, that one of his Italian commentators, Francesco Valori, calls him an "aristocratic communist."

His communism, then, which is the dominating factor in his City of the Sun, entails women's emancipation and elevation. His aristocratism, a minor factor but still a factor, keeps them from reaching the highest offices in the State.

Thus the pattern set by antiquity is repeated in the Renaissance. The position of woman in an imaginary ideal commonwealth is a mathematical function of the author's attitude toward the individual and his relation to the collective. This is a law stronger than any one thinker or any one period; it is rooted in the deepest layers of the human subconscious, in the origins of the species. Hence, obviously, we find it repeated in the next great period of Utopian thinking, in eighteenth- and nineteenth-century France.

SEVEN

The Feminine Revolution

The feminine revolution must now complete the proletarian revolution, just as the proletarian revolution has consolidated the bourgeois revolution, which, in turn, was a consequence of the philosophical revolution.

AUGUSTE COMTE[1]

As we pass from the eighteenth century into the nineteenth, the transformation of social and economic life proceeds at a pace unprecedented in the past. More changes take place in fifty years than in the three centuries that had passed since the end of the Middle Ages. Europe's population triples in the course of a single century. The masses, concentrating more and more in the large cities, engender a group-force, dynamic, explosive, new in the history of mankind.

Consider where history had brought people. The slums, where they might rot, unnoticed, in a life that was death long before death failed to liberate the souls they did not have into an after-life that did not exist; the mines, where women and six-year-old children were waning away, in eleven-hour days, feet in water, heads in coal dust, underfed, underpaid, underhoused, under-dressed; the cotton mills, for bipedal beasts of burden; the misery of the weavers, the cruelty of the poorhouses—the indus-trial revolution, with its attendant evils from which to escape, against which to react; with its attendant unlimited possibilities to believe in, to fight for, to conquer.

Both ingredients, flight and fight, went into the Utopias of the eighteenth and early nineteenth centuries. Flight into visions of faraway islands peopled by blessed primitives; fight for a new order, emerging from the ruins of the old, encompassed in ideal schemes to be *enacted here and now:* in experimental colo-nies such as Fourier's or Owen's; or on a wider, eventually uni-versal basis, by revolutionary means, such as Babeuf's.

Fear and hope, reaction and revolution, often meet on a strip of common ground: protest against the present, by escape into an irretrievable past, or by a lunge into a future which will be the present of tomorrow.

The simultaneity of forward and backward movement in eighteenth-century French thought is described by Hans Hinter-häuser:

The faith in progress, in the coming of a morally superior and better organized humanity—a faith pushed forward by Enlightenment *à pas de géant*—is thus contrasted by another element, however little apparent it may be within the whole ideal structure: a backward orientation, born of tiredness, of being fed up with civilization, of a feeling that our world is getting old. And this feeling becomes, increasingly, an integral part of eighteenth-century thought.[2]

To take liberalism on the one hand and socialism on the other, and to see in their struggle during the eighteenth and nineteenth centuries an expression of the opposition between individualism and collectivism, is, of course, erroneous, as is any oversimplification. Individualist liberalism, especially in the beginning, championed the cause of the peasants against the seigniors, of the wage earner against the capitalist exploiter, of the broad masses against the feudal overlords. And insofar as liberalism, individualist liberalism, espoused the cause of the masses, it was also in favor of women's emancipation. It is enough to remember Condorcet, unquestionably an individualist, and his untiring fight in favor of women's suffrage and the equal rights of men and women. According to him, women, just like men, are "susceptible of moral ideas and capable of reasoning from them."[3]

Another example, of course, is John Stuart Mill, with his rousing pages on *The Subjection of Women*[4]—brought about by historical contingencies, not by an intrinsic inferiority in women—and their necessary and imminent liberation.

But not all liberals who championed the Rights of Man, championed also the Rights of Woman. Far from it. Whereas *all* socialists, without exception, based their new order on the emancipation of women. Thus, after the usual caveat against oversimplifications, we see the pattern re-emerging with mathematical precision.

Fourier had a keen sense of the relativity of woman's position and character. He was the first, perhaps, to see her character as a function—I use the term in good conscience, for Fourier's was a very mathematical sort of mind—of social organization.

To judge woman's character as vicious and inferior because this is the way it seems revealed in "civilization," says Fourier, is as wrong as it would be to judge man's character in terms of the Russian serfs who know neither honor nor liberty. It would be like assuming that beavers are stupid beasts because that is what they are in captivity, whereas their teamwork, in their natural state of freedom, reveals them to be the most intelligent of all quadrupeds. Exactly the same difference exists between the women enslaved by our civilization, and the free women of the new social order to come : the *État sociétaire,* the harmonious society of the "phalanstery." In this future collective society, "women will be superior to men in industry, loyalty, and nobility." But until the establishment of this order, which will combine co-operation and liberty, woman—like a captive beaver or a Russian peasant—remains an inferior, servile, soulless, spiritless, deceitful being.[5]

To corroborate his argument, Fourier points out that women, far more frequently than men, make great rulers. "It is well known," he claims, "that out of eight sovereign, free, and unmarried women, seven have reigned gloriously; whereas there are seven weak and insignificant kings in any eight."[6] This anticipates John Stuart Mill, who, in *The Subjection of Women,* has a curious footnote on the talent of women for ruling and government. He points to the great number of women rulers (as regents for minor heirs) in Hindu history, and their outstanding efficiency.

Thus, Fourier feels fully entitled to conclude that women, in a state of liberty, will be *superior* to men "in all functions of the spirit and of the body, except insofar as they are based on brute force."[7]

We take exception to this exception. For, in a totally collectivized society, women might become men's equals, or superiors, *even in physical force*. Not only the psychological state, but also the somatic state of women is a "function" of the social order, and, in the present order of things, physical force is a symptom, not a cause, of masculine superiority. In other words, the social order has evolutionary effects on the species and transforms its physical as well as its psychological character.

But of course, Fourier could not yet know that. Dynamic though he was in everything else, he looked at the human species as static, after all.

Within his phalanstery, the contrast between the one and the many is cancelled. The interest of the individual coincides with the interest of the group. The instinctive gratification of passion coincides with rationality. Conflict is replaced by "attraction" : each for all and all for each, for this is the way the eternal geometer, *le grand ouvrier,* has ordained it. And as there is harmony between the individual and the collective, so is there harmony between men and women. As in all collective Utopias, women get the same education as men, physical, intellectual, and moral ; they share the work and they share the honors. "Women shall be the object of a reasoned veneration. No one shall enjoy higher consideration and honor than the woman who, through her work and merit, has climbed to the highest dignity of the social hierarchy."[8] The patriarchal family having been abolished, men and women are associated in free love, whose enjoyment is not curtailed by material considerations such as household cares or child rearing. These are left to the community.

Dozens of volumes have been written on women and socialism. Robert Owen's[9] collectivism is reflected in his heavy emphasis on environment, as against heredity, in determining the character of the individual. It is embodied in his "villages of co-operation," a sort of *Kolkhoz* or *kibbutz* where agriculture is industrialized and competition is replaced by co-operation. All property being held in common, and household and kitchen, child care and school being communal, women are men's free and equal partners in work, in love, in government.

Much has been written on the feminism of Henri de Saint-Simon[10] and his school. Enfantin,[11] his disciple, recounts the story, told by so many socialists, of how woman, enslaved by society, "gradually rises to a position nearer man's, and acquires with every day that passes more influence upon the social order; how the causes that, up till now, have determined her subaltern position, have gradually diminished, to the point of disappearing altogether; and how, consequently, this domination, this tutelage, this eternal minority, still today imposed on women, is bound to disappear, too, inasmuch as it would be incompatible with the social order which we foresee."

Olinde Rodrigues, another disciple of Saint-Simon, expands this feminism into a new thesis, basing it on an alleged saying of his master, according to which "man and woman together make up the social individual"—"*Voilà pourquoi l'homme et la femme, sont l'individu social!*"[12]—which seems to echo Kant: "Only together man and woman form a complete and whole human being; the one sex complements the other."

In a work called *Saint Jean de la femme,* Enfantin goes so far as to anticipate the coming of a woman messiah. Men are but "the companions of women," and "there could be neither peace nor social justice without the preponderance of women"!

There is one among the French Utopians of the eighteenth century whom we should single out: Foigni, who went farther than the others. If the others postulated, as the basis for their communistic order, the emancipation of women and their equality with men in all things—the minimization, that is, of sexual differences—Foigni anticipates the conclusions of modern biology in asserting that there can be no total collectivization, no complete communism, as long as present reproductive habits are maintained. In his completely communistic commonwealth,[13] there are, in fact, no men or women; all inhabitants are of the same sex, being both male and female at the same time.

He took the idea from a prophetess and quietist, Antoinette Bourignon, who wrote numerous religious pamphlets in French, Flemish, and German during the seventeenth century. According to her, the distinction between the sexes is a consequence of sin. In a perfect society—ruled by total altruism, with a community of goods—this distinction would disappear.[14]

Foigni looked with pity and contempt on the one-sexed halfmen of our world. In Austral Land, man is made in the image of God. One of them is enough to procreate; and when Foigni hears from a traveler—the usual device in these eighteenth-century Utopias—a description of this sort of perfect human being, he "could not help remembering what our Christian theology teaches regarding the generation of the Second Person of the Holy Trinity."

The more perfect a being, the less will he be wanting in order to act. If the concurrence of two is needed to complete one single action, this action cannot be without very great defects, because it requires the combination of two actions for only one effect. These two actions can hardly ever be perfectly co-ordinated; and, one preceding the other in time or having more force than the other, there ensues conflict, delay, and compromise, and this necessarily will cause a great number of defects in the thing created.

Conflict, delay, and compromise, which ruin not only the generation of offspring, but society as a whole, are thus eliminated from Austral Land; there the perfection of the group coincides with the perfection of the individual, who, in his perfection, can be neither male nor female, which are both defective.

The same modern biological implication of total collectivism was drawn by an English author of the nineteenth century, W. H. Hudson. The perfect collective of his Crystal Age[15] is based on the system of the beehive with its queen bee. Lewis Mumford sums up:

The crystallites have done away with the difficulties of mating by appointing one woman, in every house, to be the house-mother, the woman whose capital duty is to carry on the family; the entire burden of each generation falls upon her shoulders, and in return for the sacrifice she is treated with the respect due to divinity. . . . The wish of a house-mother is a command; the word of the house-mother is law. . . . For all except the house-mother, sex is a matter of purely physical appearance. . . . The social life of the household is not to be wrecked by the storms and stresses of the individual's passions. The engines of life are no longer dangerous: the fuel has been taken away! A chill moonlight felicity is all that remains.[16]

Bisexuality, in one case, specialization of the reproductive function, in the other: these are two instances, the earliest we know of, where total altruism and collectivism are associated with a change in the reproductive habits of the species.

Let us now look at "individualism," insofar as it links the affirmation of the rights of the individual with class privileges, and rejects the rights of the "masses." Let us test the action of this individualism on the graph representing the Ascent of Woman, depressing though such a test may be.

Of Rousseau, we remember his influence on the Revolution, on the drafting of the Rights of Man. We tend to forget how little he thought of the "unknown" or "despised" multitudes; how he thought the rule of the people an absurdity. For Rousseau, the prerequisites for democracy are too many ever to exist. "If there were a nation of gods, it could be governed democratically. So perfect a government is unsuited to men."[17]

Rousseau favors an *elective aristocracy* as the best form of government. "In a word," he says, "it is the best and most natural order of things that the wisest should govern the multitude." And the wisest, according to him, are the richest—in most cases, if not always.

Liberty, not being a fruit suited to all climates, is not within the reach of all people.

What is, logically, his attitude toward women?

In the family it is clear, for several reasons which lie in its very nature, that the father ought to command. In the first place, the authority ought not to be equally divided between father and mother; the government must be single, and in every division of opinion there must be one preponderant voice to decide. Secondly, however lightly we may regard the disadvantages peculiar to women, yet, as they necessarily occasion intervals of inaction, this is a sufficient reason for excluding them from this supreme authority. ... Besides, the husband ought to be able to superintend his wife's conduct, because it is of importance for him to be assured that the children, whom he is obliged to acknowledge and maintain, belong to no one but himself.[18]

Rousseau's ideas as to how girls should be educated to make submissive, sweet wives, apt to assure the peace and happiness of their husbands, confirms, more or less, those expressed by Fenelon,[19] in his famous treatise on the education of girls, which were bitterly criticized by Fourier.

A thinker—probably unique—who oscillates from the extremes of a collectivist ideal to those of individualism, is

Diderot. He wanders from the postulate of a communist order, based on a community of goods, to a Nietzschean, super-individualist anarchism, based on a contempt for the rabble—*les êtres communs,* who remain always the same throughout history, as opposed to *les âmes fortes.*

A graph of this oscillation would correspond exactly to one of his oscillating attitude toward women.

In his primitive-communistic paradise of Tahiti, the women are wonderfully free and enjoy the same rights as men. "Woman's features, her looks, her posture, are not at all like those of civilized women,"[20] who are corrupt and subdued. The Tahitian women are strong, beautiful, proud and innocent. They do men's jobs. There is a Grand Priestess, honored all over the island. Love is free: women offer themselves even to strangers stranded on their shores; for such freedom favors the increase of population, and such increase is the highest good. The Tahitian women, however, seem to outnumber their men; at least, this seems to follow from the explanation the "Old Tahitian" offers to the French chaplain, on whom he urges the love of the women and girls. "The number of our women and girls is too great for that of our men."

Here we would have a first hint of the connection between rising population and the prevalence of women.

Diderot, also considers ethics a function, in the mathematical sense, of population density. The morals of an overpopulated country are one thing; those of an underpopulated country, quite another. "Are the ethical laws governing the people of Tahiti better or worse than yours?" the Old Tahitian asks the Frenchman. "The question is easy to answer: Does your country contain more people than it can nourish? In this case your morals in your country are as good as our morals in our country. Could it feed a greater population than it actually contains? In this case our morals would be superior to yours."

In this connection between population dynamics and ethical

system—which affects and reflects character—Diderot anticipates the most modern theories.

Another aspect of Diderot's collectivist way of thinking is his
statistical conception of happiness and unhappiness. "It has often
occurred to me," he says, "that the sum of good and of evil is
variable for each individual; but that the well-being and suffering of any one species stay within limits that cannot be
changed." This he wrote a good two hundred years before any-
body knew about the indeterminateness of the atom in a mass
governed by strict laws of behavior!

To the extent that he was a collectivist thinker, Diderot was
pro-feminine. But there were times when he yielded to sudden
outbursts of individualism and became, despite the genuine
communism of his Tahitian Utopia, a dogged defender of
private property. As far as man's private property is concerned,
he writes, "each one is at the head of his property: a portion of
the general wealth of which he is the exclusive and absolute
master; over which he is king, and which he may use or misuse
at his own discretion."[21]

Inasmuch as he is an individualist, a man of the *ancien
régime,* he considers woman as an inferior being, against whom
nature and civilization have formed a most cruel alliance.

In his essay *"Sur les femmes,"* from which we had occasion
to quote in Chapter II, Diderot projects, as it were, his own
ambiguous attitude toward womanhood onto the female character itself, which he describes as "extreme in force and in weakness, beautiful like Klopstock's Seraphim; terrible like Milton's
Satan."

The strong individualistic component of Diderot's thought
anticipates, and has often been compared with, Friedrich
Nietzsche's way of thinking.[22] In Nietzsche, however, there was
no ambivalence with regard either to crowds or women.

Woman, according to Nietzsche, is a domestic animal: tender and often gracious, uneducable, hiding a tiger's claw under a velvet glove; the toy of his superman. One might call her "intelligent," if intelligence means shrewdness in exploiting practical situations; but she has no "sentiment," if sentiment means depth, which appertains only to man.

It does not appertain to those men, however, who, more flat-minded than women, strive for her emancipation and equality with men, who want her to degenerate to the point of "general education," or, worse yet, to reading newspapers and talking politics. As if there could be anything more ludicrous and more ridiculous to a profound, philosophical man than an enlightened woman! Those who want to "cultivate" women are donkeys who make them ever more hysterical and unfit for their only rightful job, which is to bear children. No, woman should be as she always has been; and if you go to see one, don't forget the whip.

But then, what Nietzsche sought certainly was not the liberation of the masses, nor even the happiness of man, but his elevation to the dizzy, isolated heights of the superman. Never has there been a more fanatical individualist; never one in whose imaginary world women fared as badly.

But his voice rang loud because it rang lonely. The anti-feminists were losing out; their ranks were thinning. The Ascent of Woman was in full course; so was, to some extent, and in certain ways, the Descent of Man.

This shift—and this is the gist of what we are trying to demonstrate in this book—is part of a wider, more comprehensive shift, described penetratingly by Erich Kahler:

Evolution, as I have attempted to show, is a process of extension of scope. Now in the course of this process it happened at certain points that the emphasis, the points of gravity of events, shifted from one level to another. Just as with the emergence of *Homo sapiens,* the emphasis has moved from body to mind, and evolution proper has turned into human history, in a similar way, in our age, since the nineteenth century, the point of gravity of events appears to have shifted from the individual to the collective level. And while on the collective level, man has immensely expanded his reach, the individual, through this very process, has shrunk in independence, self-regulation, power of control, and range of knowledge. The fact that the technological and intellectual scope of humanity has advanced far beyond the capacity of the individual mind, and that individual consciousness is less and less able to keep pace with the growing extent and complexity of happenings and with what I would call collective consciousness—namely, the vast corpus of our present, evermoving, everchanging knowledge— this tragic inadequacy of the individual is one of the basic causes of our human crisis.[23]

This is the full context of women's rise and emancipation during the nineteenth and twentieth centuries: the crisis of the individual, and the "shift of emphasis" from the individual to the collective.

Into this crisis Marxism inserted itself, as cause and effect; its connection with the rise of woman was understood by the Marxists more fully than by any other school of thought.

This does not make us Marxists. We need not believe in the class struggle, an infiltration of pseudo-Darwinian origin, disproved by history and biology alike. Nor need we believe in materialism and in systems of production as the prime movers and sole causes of historical change. Modern science has taught us that the interrelations between matter and energy, or ideas, are far more complicated than the Marxists, in their time, could possibly have imagined. Needless to repeat: the course of economic and social history in the New World totally belies Marx's prophecies, and the mental acrobatics of his epigoni, in an effort to stretch the old theory to cover new fields, are rather pitiful to behold.

Yet if we consider materialistic communism—the abolition of private property and the communalization of the means of production—as an important aspect of collectivism in a wider sense, then the Marxist insight and foresight with regard to woman's role becomes plausible. Plausible, the enormous space reserved to the woman problem in Marxist literature and the influence of this literature on the emancipation movement; plausible, also, the important role played by women in the history of the Marxist socialist revolutions.

In his *Origin of the Family, Private Property, and the State,* Engels, as did other Marxists after him, accepts in full the theory—first proposed by Bachofen on the basis of mythological and archeological research, and then adopted by Morgan on the basis of anthropological research—that a matriarchal and/or matrilinear order preceded the patriarchal one all over the world. In Engels' view, of course, the superior position of womanhood is based on the community of property. "The validity of the matriarchal law," says another Marxist, August Bebel, in his enormously influential book, *Woman and Socialism,* "means communism. The rise of the patriarchal law means the rise and rule of private property. Patriarchal law signifies, at the same time, the subjection and enslavement of women."[24] Just as matriarchy was once rooted in prehistoric communism, so will the future liberation of women be part and parcel of the communist revolution and the abolition of property.

Thus Marx and Engels, in the *Communist Manifesto:*

On what foundation is the present family, the bourgeois family, based? On capital, on private gain. In its completely developed form this family exists only among the bourgeoisie. But this state of things finds its complement in the practical absence of the family among the proletarians, and in public prostitution.

The bourgeois family will vanish as a matter of course, when its complement vanishes, and both will vanish with the vanishing of capital.

It is a different question whether or not the Bachofen-Morgan theory can stand its ground in the light of more recent research. A target for violent opposition from the beginning —as is any new theory, for that matter—it has not been corroborated by subsequent research among aborigines in Africa and Australia. Specialists have unearthed many facts that would not fit any theory at all: just facts. They have done that in every field; it was the fashion, in the recent past. Quite recently, however, depth psychologists like Erich Neumann and scholars like Sophie Drinker have stressed the importance of the female component in the depths of the collective subconscious as well as in the depths of the origins of human organization.

And even if Bachofen's great work does abound in misinterpretations of facts, and Morgan's is based on material that is considered too restricted today, it is generally acknowledged that woman's role in pre-individual society—as provider, as healer, as priestess and witch, as pivot, at any rate, of social organization—was considerably more important than the one she played in later times.

So the Marxist position on the original connection of feminism and communism, if inadequate, is not wrong; just as the Marxist prophecy concerning society is not wrong, but inadequate.

For one thing, the Marxists shied away from their own logical conclusions. Unlike the Utopian communists, who courageously prophesied the total abolition of the family in an indeterminate somewhere-sometime, the Marxists felt committed to action in the here-and-now. They had to appeal to men and women who loved their families and wanted happiness for them, not their abolition. They had to defend themselves against the accusation, "But you communists would introduce community of women," screamed, according to the *Communist Manifesto,* by "the whole bourgeoisie in chorus." So they promised to abolish the family only insofar as it was a bourgeois family based on, and poisoned by, economic interests. By abolishing property, by transferring the material burdens and responsibilities of the single household to the community and freeing women for productive labor on an equal footing with men, monogamy, based on free but lasting affection between man and woman, would not only not be abolished, but would, at last, become a reality. This added a romantic touch to the Marxist program.

However, since the position of woman, though undoubtedly connected with the economic system, is not based on it alone, the communist promise was bound to fail, to some extent. The progress of womanhood in communist countries, especially during the early phases, has been spectacular. But there has also been, especially in later phases, confusion and reaction, a new emphasis on family and motherhood—and an acknowledgment of failure, as exemplified by A. V. Nemilov's *The Biological Tragedy of Woman.*[25]

This Soviet author sadly admits that, in spite of all the constitutional and institutional advantages offered to women by the Soviet State, they have not reached equality with men. This he ascribes to motherhood, with its contingent rewards and drawbacks. This is a point of view that seems to take us back to the thesis that "anatomy is destiny," which, in different contexts, stresses the importance of genetic inheritance over environment, of the individual over the group—a strictly un-Marxian way of thinking.

That Marxism as a philosophy of history is inadequate and full of contradictions is no news. The treatment of the woman question is just another example, if one were needed.

What is important from our point of view is the conscious

and constant identification of collectivism, even if understood as
materialistic communism, which is merely one of its aspects,
with the emancipation of women, even if this emancipation, in
a context of incomplete premises, was bound to remain incomplete.

The feminist-collectivist passages in Marxist literature are
indeed so many and so well-known that we need not repeat them
here. Suffice it to remember Marx's observation in a letter to
Kugelmann in 1868, that "Social progress can be measured with
precision by the social position of the female sex." And Lenin:
"It is impossible to win the masses for politics, unless we include
the women. . . . We must win the millions of working women
in city and village for our cause, for our struggle, and in particular, for the communistic transformation of society. Without
the women there can be no true mass movement."[26]

But there can be no true mass movement without men, either;
and if the Ascent of Woman were really to be paid for with
the Descent of Man, we wouldn't want to buy it.

The disintegration of the individual is quite possible today.

Begin from the outside. You can change a man's eyes, graft-
ing parts of another man's eyes onto his. You can change his
arms, his legs, his heart. You may put the heart into his leg,
even, if you wish. You can cut him up and put him together
again the way one can cut up certain sponges; let the minute
component parts swim freely in the water, and, lo! they will
swim together and re-form an individual: is it the same? a new
one? Science is relearning what nature had unlearned. You may
put a man in the deep freeze and revive him at will. "Death," a
Soviet scientist recently said, "is a sickness we are learning to
cure." An individual that can be cured of death, certainly, is
different from a common mortal individual.

You can operate on a man's brain, altering his character, his temperament. You can feed a drug to a "criminal" and make him over as a decent man. You can feed another drug to a sane man and turn him into a schizophrenic. You can brainwash the one and the many, manipulate their tastes, their beliefs, their wills. You may turn their innermost out, and their deepest past up, and project the result into an outside world, which is no longer the outside world of two or three generations ago.

All that has been discovered about the interaction between group psychology and individual psychology, between environment and heredity, between physical action and psychical action, tends to undermine the concept of the individual.

Certainly, the emphasis has shifted from the individual to the collective : but the individual must eventually evolve together with the collective. The *involution* of the individual would disintegrate the collective : as happens, eventually, in every totalitarian State. The body crumbles when the cells decay. The totalitarian State, therefore, is strictly anti-evolutionary. New paths will be tried. The crisis of the individual, as any crisis, is necessarily temporary.

To see how collective evolution—after the crisis provoked by the "shift"—necessarily implies individual evolution, let us look at two examples.

One is provided by industrial evolution, which, as the Marxists knew, is in many respects the nucleus or pattern of social evolution in general.

Begin with the arts and crafts. Every worker is a master who knows and loves his craft. He buys the raw materials, he owns his tools. He conceives, designs his product, makes it, finishes it in all its parts and aspects, tests it, finds it good, and sells it. A whole man. A rounded individual.

Then comes the machine, which competes with the artisan, defeats him, drives him into unemployment, where he loses his craft, becomes de-individualized. When the artisan is absorbed by the factory, he functions, himself, as a piece of machinery. He turns the same handle day in, day out. Of a thousand objects unknown to him, he knows only a thousand times one screw, which he turns, in a thousand dreary moments, on the assembly line. His individuality is warped. The shift from the individual to the collective has taken place.

But, at the same time, something else is taking place. The evolution of the collective takes its own course. The collective expands; it gains in complexity. The machines grow ever more complicated. Their manipulation demands an ever-increasing skill. There are fewer and fewer places for the unskilled laborer, who becomes a left-over, created by an earlier phase of industrial evolution.

Insofar as he is integrated into the industrial process, the new workingman is rapidly advancing in skill—individuality—until the day will come, not far off, when all workingmen, to use Adriano Olivetti's phrase, will be scientists.

He may be a scientist, one may object, and yet be a warped individual.

But the labor psychologists and statisticians assure us that a skilled worker who in his spare time reads the Great Books, decorates his living room with reproductions of paintings from the Guggenheim collection, sings in a choir, and plays a role in plant management, will produce more per working hour than one without such outside interests. Thus, the more progressive the industrial management, the more outlets of this sort will it offer to its workingmen who, according to all accustomed standards, are in no way inferior, as individuals, to the guild masters of former times.

And yet . . . There is no need to insist. Obviously, the new individual is not the same as the old one. The point we wish to make is that industrial development provides a striking example of how the evolution of the collective, after the crisis of the individual, depends on, runs parallel with, the evolution of the individual.

Just as Marx sought his pattern for society and social development in the factory and industrial development, so did Freud use the army and its psychology as a pattern for social psychology in general.

The army and its development thus provides another example to prove our point. We begin with the armored knight, to whom the kings of old entrusted the business of warfare. Whether on horseback or on foot, they were strong, they were skilled, those knights.

Then came the cannon, the machine gun, and the general draft. Masses of unprofessional, unskilled soldiers : cannon fodder, de-individualized. Here, in this particular context, is the crisis of the individual. But then the organization grows in complexity; the machinery it depends upon becomes ever more complicated. Military service becomes a school, a long, highly technical training. The pilot, the commando, the marine of to-day, need more individual initiative and skill than did the armed knight of old.

That, with the obsolescence of war, the army as a social organism has also grown obsolete, is a different problem. The evolution of the collective, at any rate, as long as it could go on, implied the evolution of the individual.

This granted it must be added that the shift of emphasis from the individual to the collective implies other shifts as well. It implies a shift from competition to co-operation as the basic factor of evolution. The awareness of this shift is already evident in Darwin himself.

The Origin of Species reflects its own epoch: an epoch of enterprise and conquest, of profit and misery, of alarming expansion, of unbridled individualism. Woe to the vanquished;

the pitiless struggle for life and the survival of the fittest became the only recognizable law of nature, to which man, too, had to conform lest he succumb in a world based upon mutual extermination.

In the *Descent of Man* Darwin knew better. He pointed out how, in innumerable cases, the struggle among individuals for the means of existence ceases, and how that struggle is replaced by co-operation, which secures to the species the best conditions for survival. He recognizes that in all such cases the fittest are neither the strongest nor the slyest, but those who learn to combine so as to support each other mutually, strong and weak alike, for the well-being of the community. "This is true Darwinism," wrote another British naturalist, W. Bates. "It is horrible what they have made of Darwin." With these words Bates encourages Kropotkin, as the latter reports, to elaborate his theory of mutual aid as a factor in evolution.[27]

Then came Espinas, Alverdes, Wheeler, Allee, and a host of modern experimental biologists, who tested and proved this thesis in nature and laboratory: a theory that reflects our age, and the age to come.

Struggle is not a primary phenomenon in the evolution of life. "It presupposes already a certain amount of organization," Allee points out, that is, "defense of territory and the establishment and the maintenance of social dominance often call for hard fighting between the individuals. . . . This aspect of intraspecies struggle appears on the evolutionary scale later than does primitive automatic co-operation."[28]

Struggle is not primary. It is a mid-evolutionary phenomenon, leading, often, to the formation of higher organisms, after which it becomes dis-functional, anti-evolutionary. Co-operation takes the upper hand.

Whether we are aware of it or not, we have just entered into such a phase. And "the weight of the evidence from the sociology of other animals strongly indicates that, despite many appearances to the contrary, human altruistic drives are as firmly based on our animal ancestry as is man himself. Despite many well-known appearances to the contrary, human goodness, on the personal, community, national, and international levels, is as natural as is man's trend toward intelligence."[29]

The shift from the individual to the collective, from struggle to co-operation, implies—as we saw in Chapter I—a shift of emphasis from the masculine to the feminine. Insofar as evolution proceeds through co-operation, it proceeds through the female. Group-making from the beginning, the female thrives on the forces which the group, in turn, releases. "This phase of the social implications of sex has escaped general comment," writes Warder Allee.[30]

"Masculine" virtues, indeed, appear sadly antiquated today. The aggressive type becomes a Don Quixote or a gangster. All the qualities that Plutarch, Fénelon, and Rousseau recommended as the basis for the education of girls, today are urged, are forced, upon mankind in general. Sweet manners, unselfishness, loyalty, submissiveness. A rather radical reassessment or transformation of moral and social values has taken place. The feminine components in each one's individual mind and structure, and in the mind and structure of the collective, have acquired a new pre-eminence.

This is what we mean by the Feminine Revolution, the Ascent of Woman.

How far it has gone, and how far it may go, we shall see in the concluding chapters.

EIGHT

Ascent of Woman
Lower Reaches

Woman is not a completed reality, but rather a becoming, and it is in her becoming that she should be compared with man; that is to say, her possibilities should be defined. What gives rise to much of the debate is the tendency to reduce her to what she has been, to what she is today, in raising the question of her capabilities; for the fact is that capabilities are clearly manifested only when they have been realized—but the fact is also that when we have to do with a being whose nature is transcendent action, we can never close the books.

SIMONE DE BEAUVOIR[1]

They were Utopians, dreamers, detached from this world. But Leonardo da Vinci, too, was a Utopian when he dreamed up the airplane, as were many after him.

At the beginning of this century, there was a famous physicist, a learned padre, who taught school in Florence.

"When shall we be able to fly like the birds, Father, we, too?" one of his students asked him.

The padre shook his head and smiled condescendingly. "Never, my dear fellow, never. It is a vicious circle. The more power we need, the heavier the weight we have to put up with. The law of gravitation is stronger than we, and will always be so."

The student, Corrado Tumiati, didn't really give a hoot for flying, he tells us in his book, *Nessuno Risponde*. "But for being free, yes. Ignorant schoolboy that I was, I did not know what to answer. And so I slid silently through the heavy entrance door into school, with my nostalgia. Like a mouse into its hole."[2]

The Utopians' dreams about the Ascent of Woman have been like the Utopians' dreams about the ascent of the airplane. Against all odds, they have come true.

What were those dreams made of?

Equal educational opportunities for boys and girls.

Health and physical strength, for women as for men. Which, in turn, means a new look, a reappraisal of the aesthetic feminine ideal.

Work for all women as for all men.

Equal rights and equal duties for men and women.

A de-emphasis of motherhood as the only scope of a woman's life.

Rationalization of procreation.

De-emphasis of the single home; emphasis on community services.

Let us briefly examine the position of women in five countries —Italy, the United States, Israel, the Soviet Union, and China —in an effort to understand why these positions are as they are.

Equality of educational opportunities, of course, is the runway for the Ascent of Woman.

In Italy, this runway exists. There is no longer any discussion about that. Coeducation and common curriculum are taken for granted—much more so than in the United States, where discussion of the usefulness of special curricula for girls and women is still current and unresolved. More than a divergence in the concept of women, this reflects a divergence in the concept of education. For the Italian, education is still classical education in the liberal arts, education of the mind. Thus, it is the same for boys and girls. For the American, education is largely vocational; it is, furthermore, not of the mind only but of "the whole man," "the whole woman." Hence, woman's education is supposed to be different, preparing the girl not only for a job but for homemaking and motherhood.

Plato would be pleased at entering a classroom in Florence —a town as splendid as his Athens—and seeing the boys and girls studying his dialogues. The girls make up about one third of the class. They occupy one row of desks. The boys occupy the other two. The boys wear coats or sweaters, ties or open shirts. The girls wear, winter and summer, a sort of black apron frock, knee length, with long sleeves and a high neckline, to check any tendency to sport tight sweaters or deep décolletés, and to shield them, in any case, from the concupiscent looks of the boys.

Plato is puzzled. There must be something fundamentally wrong in Florence-Athens.

"We never meant," the first girl reads in halting Greek, "when we constructed the State, that the opposition of natures should extend to every difference. . . ."

As she reads "opposition of natures," some of the boys begin to giggle. In the last row, one boy waves a sheet of paper with *"Evviva la piccola differenza"* ("Three cheers for the little difference") written on it in large block letters.

"There is nothing peculiar in the construction of women, which would affect them in the administration of the State," the girl continues. Here she gets stuck. "Skip it," the Professor says. "Sit down. A 'two' on your report card. Insufficient preparation."

The girl does not know whether to laugh or to cry. Crying, for girls, is not bad style. On the other hand, the whole thing is so irrelevant. If a girl flunks, it is, by God, no tragedy. She has, let us hope, better things to do in life than work. She'll get married. Now, if a boy flunks, that is a tragedy. It means the loss of a year as a breadwinner. It indicates, furthermore, a lack of seriousness, of responsibility.

So the runway is there, in Florence-Athens; but it is incommensurate to the traffic it has to bear. A large part of it is falling into disuse and going to pieces. Education may be common and yet not equal; because the relationships between teachers and boy students are not quite the same as those between teachers and girl students; because the relationships between parents and daughters are not the same as those between parents and sons; because the relationships between boy students and girl students are not based on comradeship but on flirtation; because for the girl student the purpose of studying is to be "educated," to make a good showing as an upper-class wife, while the purpose of the boy's studying is to make a living.

Italian education—for boys and girls—consists of five years of elementary school, three years of lower high school, five years of upper high school, and four years of university.

During the first eight years the girls do notably better than the boys. They are quicker, more attentive, more orderly in manners and minds. The boys are more confused, less adjustable to classroom discipline—which is severe, from kindergarten on— more liable to nervous disorders such as stammering, less enduring in their efforts, more erratic. After the eighth year of school, a change sets in. The boys catch up with the girls, then outdo them. On entering the university, boys, on the average, produce work that is more creative, more original, more distinguished, than that of girls.

This "curve" of girl students' achievements coincides, it would seem, with the curve of women's attainments in academic careers.

Women teachers make up 73 per cent of the faculties of elementary schools in Italy, 62 per cent in the lower high schools, 48 per cent in the upper high schools, 5.7 per cent in the universities! An interesting curve, which, of course, does not reflect "biological destiny," but merely an early phase in the Ascent of Woman. That it may be changed within the course of one single generation has been demonstrated, for instance, in Russia. To this we shall return later.

In Italy the schools are open to all, regardless of sex. Fees are nominal, amounting to about twenty or twenty-five dollars a year. But books are costly and numerous; in fact, prohibitive. Other obstacles concurring, the sad fact is that average school attendance is 4.13 years for boys, and 3.48 years for girls.

Only 2.5 per cent of the boys, and 1.4 per cent of the girls graduate from the university.[3] These figures could be integrated
with many others to corroborate what is already clear from the
above: while education, altogether, is still a privilege of the elite
in Italy, girls do not make full use of the educational opportunities they do have.

Why not?

The ideal of the Italian woman is not to be man's equal. The
Church teaches that woman has been created for man, and that
man is the head of the family even as Christ is the head of the
Church. The Constitution of 1948 decrees equality for men and
women before the law; but the validity of this constitutional
law is overridden by older, still valid provisions of the civil code,
and by custom, which is stronger than any law.

Italian women have the right to vote and to be elected to
public offices, just like men. But to take part in political discussion is considered strictly unfeminine. If women vote, they do
not vote according to personal convictions but according to the
advice given by husband or father confessor.

After the war, when the resistance movement—a highly integrated movement in which the Communists constituted the most
efficient organizing element—brought a lot of women to the
fore,* forty-three women were elected to Parliament, constituting 4.7 per cent of the total number of elected deputies. With
the return to normalcy, the number of women in Parliament has
gone down. Thirty-four were elected in 1953 (4.1 per cent of

---

* Seventy thousand women were enlisted in the Organization for the Defense
of Women *(Gruppi di difesa della donna)*; 35,000 women fought in the ranks
of the partisans; 4,650 of these partisan women were arrested, tortured,
court-martialed by the Fascists; 2,750 were deported to Germany; 1,750 were
decorated after the war; 15 were awarded gold medals, the higest military
honor in Italy. Two thousand seven hundred and fifty partisan women were
shot or fell in battle. Five hundred and twelve held the rank of commissioned
officers in the partisan army. A remarkable record![4]

the total number of deputies), and only twenty-three in 1958 (2.6 per cent). In municipal administrations the number of women is even smaller, and it is still decreasing. At present, only 1.5 per cent of elected municipal officials are women.

An enterprising young woman lawyer of Milan recently offered herself for a judge's position that was open. The ministry rejected her candidacy because it would have run counter to "judiciary order" if a woman had obtained the job. The candidate protested the unconstitutionality of this rejection. The Council of State upheld the opinion of the ministry and rejected the candidate's protest as "evidently unfounded." The candidate, finally, carried her protest up to the Supreme Court where, at last, she won her case. In the meantime, however, the job had gone to a man.

Women until quite recently were barred from jury duty and to some extent still are. Women are barred from diplomatic careers.

In a recent parliamentary debate on the constitutionality of barring women from juries, a Christian Democratic Deputy did not blush, but was quite pleased with himself as he said:

I am not a misogynist, and it is on this account that I don't want women in the juries. Just for the love and the respect I have for them. If we admit them to jury duty, the next thing they'll want is to do military service as well. Just imagine a twenty-year-old girl getting drafted, telling her fiancé, "I passed. Mountain artillery." The fiancé, maybe has been rejected. They'll lose all their poetry, all their sweetness. I don't want my wife in the mountain artillery, nor my sister, nor my mother—and I don't want them in the juries either! [Applause from the Center and the Right.]

It seems incredible that the Italian Supreme Court has recently confirmed the validity of an old law, in blatant contradiction to the Constitution, providing a double standard of judgment for adultery. Adultery on the part of the husband is not an offense; but on the part of the wife, it is considered a crime. The adulterous wife may be arrested, prosecuted, and sent to jail—even if she had previously obtained a decree of legal separation from her adulterous husband. Since there is no divorce in Italy, she is still his wife, and he is still able to send her to jail.

The Italian man's ideal of womanhood is inspired by two traditions: the classical Roman, and the Christian romantic.

The classical Roman tradition recalls an ideal woman, *mulier,* who *domum servavit et lanam fecit*—kept house and spun wool —a concept that made of her not a slave but a queen in that particular kingdom which was enclosed within her four walls. To rule efficiently, this "queen" had to be endowed with all the gifts of a ruler: with administrative wisdom and taste, pedagogical talents, and, naturally, tenderness and absolute fidelity. This ideal of the Roman wife is still very much alive in the minds of many Italian men of strong temperament, men who are hard workers, who want to find at home peace, leisure, and beauty. In actuality, of course, the ideal is flouted more often than not, as the result of an economic reality that shrinks the little kingdom to limits which do not allow satisfaction either to the ruling "queen" or to the homecoming "king."

The Christian-chivalric-romantic tradition upholds a feminine ideal embodied, in the Catholic religion, by the Virgin Mother and, in literature, by such radiant figures as Dante's Beatrice or Petrarch's Laura. The more earthly virtues of the Roman *mulier* are replaced, in this conception, by more spiritual ones, such as beauty and feminine grace, virtues catering to the aesthetic and sentimental needs of men, for whom woman represents, as it were, an escape from the practical banalities of everyday life. This concept of woman is still very frequently met among Italian men, especially among intellectuals and artists or, more generally, among men of sensitive or religious, sometimes naïve, inclinations.

Italian literature offers vast source material for the study of the Italian man's Christian-chivalric-romantic conception of woman. After Dante and Petrarch we find it embodied in Manzoni's *Betrothed* in the innocent faithful Lucia; in Fogazzaro's sensual, restless and tormented Catholic heroines; in Verga's patient and faithful women—a fascinating type of idealized and dramatic high-class "lady."

In contemporary literature, especially among left-wing writers, a new ideal of woman is beginning to assert itself: the less prejudiced, less mysterious wife or fiancée of the workingman, a worker in her own right, a more real woman, a life- and work-companion. But we are only at the beginning of this development.

The participation of women in the Italian economic process presents a most peculiar, almost unique curve. During the first five decades of this century the curve dipped. There was a marked decrease in feminine labor. This was due to a series of special circumstances, particularly the transformation of agriculture from large landed estates, worked by hired farm labor—largely furnished by women—to direct, small-scale farming by farmer-proprietors. This transformation has been called by Italian economists the "de-proletarization of farming." We are not surprised to find that it went hand in hand with a "defeminization." Although the general "flight from the country" was as noticeable in Italy as it was in many other countries, the decrease of masculine labor was only 2.5 per cent between 1900 and 1950, whereas feminine labor dropped as much as 35 per cent!

Another factor in the dipping curve was the transition, in the northern urban centers, from a prevalence of light industries, such as textiles, which traditionally employed a large percentage of women, to machine and heavy industries, employing men.

A third factor was the appearance of laws protecting female labor—limiting hours, guaranteeing minimum wages—which made it less attractive for employers to hire women when men could be hired for almost the same price.

Thus, the relatively high percentage of female labor at the beginning of the century, on the lowest levels of employment, reflects the primitive state of the Italian economy at that time and the backwardness of its social order. In terms of population dynamics, it reflects a "tradition-directed" population with a high growth potential (high birth rate, high death rate). The decrease in female labor indicates social progress; it indicates a transition from "tradition-directedness" to "inner-directedness."

While this trend was still on, however, it began to be countered by another one: industrialization, urbanization, *collectivization;* a trend toward lower birth rates and death rates—as was shown clearly by the 1961 census—a trend toward "other-directedness." With this came a sharp rise in female labor. Between 1954 and 1960, feminine industrial labor increased by 38 per cent, while masculine labor, during the same period, showed an increase of only 32.5 per cent. In other nonagricultural activities, women have gained 30.6 per cent, men, 26.2 per cent; even in agriculture there has been a new increase of about 29 per cent in female labor, whereas male labor has decreased by 18.8 per cent.

Women thus constitute, at this moment, 27 per cent of the total labor force in Italy; not a very low figure in comparison with the American (33 per cent), but low in comparison with those of the communist countries (about 45 per cent).

It should immediately be added that the female income in Italy is much lower than in the United States where, during the top year for women's employment, 1955, women earned as much as 22.2 per cent of the national income. Women, in Italy, do not constitute an economic power; they are mostly employed in humble positions as unskilled or semi-skilled workers. The middle and upper classes, which make the intellectual weather, are as yet very little affected by the new trend. Only one out of seven middle-class women works in Italy.

The Italian middle-class home is, indeed, not organized for a working woman. Most of the services furnished in more advanced communities from outside, have to be taken care of within the home: laundering, ironing, sewing. This is only partially due to lack of facilities. There are public laundries. There are ready-made clothes. But the Italian middle-class woman does not believe in them. The laundry would come home loaded with germs if you sent it out, she says. Clothes don't fit unless you try them on three or four times. The Italian middle-class housewife often suffers from a "Penelope complex"—as an Italian psychiatrist recently put it—with all its ensuing frustrations and bereavements.

Husband and children are home for lunch, a heavy meal, long to prepare and long to digest. The children, who are much more dependent than in more advanced communities, take up a great deal of time. They are overdressed, over-accompanied, over-supervised at play and at work. They grow up—as another Italian psychiatrist observed—with a complex of the Great Mother: the archetype of the Great Mother still survives in fragments of the Oriental and Etruscan substratum of Italian culture, and from there wreaks havoc in the Italian soul.

With the price of domestic service going up—it has now reached about sixty dollars per month, which is a good slice out of an average family income of $250—it is practically impossible for a middle-class wife to raise a family and hold a job too. Besides, her working outside the home would hurt her husband's masculine pride.

Thus, a large chunk of the nineteenth century is jutting into the twentieth. But the twentieth moves on, standardizing, mass-producing, mass-communicating; and the nineteenth-century housewife in the twentieth century finds her days emptied of meaning, her mind embittered, her feelings frustrated.

We have dwelt in some detail on the situation of the Italian woman, not simply because we happen to live in the hills of Athens-Florence, and have the spectacle before our eyes, but because it seems particularly apt to prove our point: that the Ascent of Woman is bound up with an increase of collectivism in one form or another. In Italy, women are worse off or better off according to the degree of collectivization of their situation.

Italy is certainly not a collectivist country. Not even Fascism succeeded in making it so. Fascism, in fact, did not affect the position of women in any marked way. As a collectivist movement, it did some things, such as organizing housewives' brigades, pinning decorations on women's uniforms, giving them the right to vote, de-emphasizing loyalty to the closed home and emphasizing loyalty to the State. It contributed to the unionization of women workers, raising their wages, extending to them the benefits of sickness and maternity insurances, payments for overtime work, paid vacations, and so forth, which they had never enjoyed before.

But, as an ally of the Church and catering to deep-seated local habits, Fascism also insisted that woman's place was in the home and rendered her employment outside the home more difficult.[5] The resultant of these conflicting drives was zero, and the position of women under Fascism did not undergo any notable changes.

Italian culture is humanistic, a Renaissance culture for the elite; not a mass culture, certainly. Although industrialization has taken giant steps in the last fifteen years, it is still in its beginnings. The arts and crafts, on an individualistic basis, still hold their own against the industrialization and mass production that have only begun to change the country's social structure.

Urbanization—another powerful factor of collectivization—is gaining, but slowly. Out of fifty million inhabitants, only eleven million live in communities of one hundred thousand or more. Almost four-fifths of the population are dispersed in small villages—in the mountains, often cut off from the bigger centers, with a bus that may pass twice a week, or never.

The Italian is still as much an individualist as the changing times will permit him to be : with his neighbor, with his partner, with his government—and with his wife.

This is why the Ascent of Woman is slow in Italy. But Italy will have to come to terms with collectivism—and thus, with its women, too.

[The same kind of conflicting drives we have noted in Italy under Fascism could also be observed in Nazi Germany. The patriarchal-homosexual character of its government is well-known ; so are its slogans—"back to the home," "reproduction," "womanly work," *"Kinder, Küche, Kirche."* Less well-known is the fact that this policy—except for an initial, but rather sensational success in the increase of the birth rate—resulted in complete failure. The German woman did not go back to the home ; nor did she apply herself to womanly work. On the contrary, the number of women working away from their homes—in factories, in offices, in all walks of life—and the number of women who studied in German universities, increased spectacularly. As in Italy, family ties were loosened by the early absorption of the children by the State. To this influence should be added, in Germany's case, the government's policy in favor of illegitimate motherhood, regarded by scholars of comparative law as exemplary and progressive : one more illustration of the meeting of the archaic and the revolutionary. The children born out of wedlock bore the mother's name and could inherit her possessions.

To this should be added the fact that the drain on the men by the war left the German matriarchs in key positions in many fields, and that the heavy death toll in the German army altered the sex ratio in their favor. This explains why German women were prepared to emerge after the war as a formidable power.

The Federal Republic is falling, by and large, into the American pattern of "other-directedness," the pattern of standardization and mass production: women now control twenty per cent of the entire production, with two-thirds of the feminine population gainfully employed in one way or another! Various explanations have been advanced to explain this unheralded turn toward matriarchy—which was already observable in Nazi Germany—usually, economic. According to Clifford Kirkpatrick,[6] the female labor force was indispensable, first to the rearmament program, then to the war-depleted national economy. It should be kept in mind, however, that there were seven million unemployed in Germany when the Nazis took over, and that the influx of women into the labor market and higher learning could not have occurred as promptly as it did had it occurred on purely economic grounds.

It has been observed time and again that women made good Nazis. They frequently put party interests ahead of the family, as can be seen from the number of divorces granted on the ground that the plaintiff—the wife—was a Nazi, and the defendant husband did not live up [or down] to her standards. The attractiveness of Nazism for women has been ascribed particularly to the fact that it gave them a feeling of "belonging." It increased their group or community feeling. Their devotion to the régime is another factor explaining their unheralded promotion.

In broadest terms, the contrast between the post-Nietzschean Nazi slogans about women, and their actual rise on the social and economic scale is one more illustration of the inherent contradictions of Nazi thinking. "Struggle" and "survival of the fittest," for the superman of a super-race, on the one hand; and on the other hand all this was to be had through collectivism. The individualistic part of the program remained in the realm of foggy ideas; the collectivistic part was enacted. Hence the Ascent of Woman in Germany.]

If Italy is still prevailingly individualistic, we should classify the United States as prevailingly collectivistic. Industrialization and urbanization, mechanization and standardization, equalization of tastes and aspirations, the development of a true mass culture (consumed and produced largely by women)—all these are aspects or expressions of this development. Its origin could be detected over a hundred years ago, when Tocqueville wrote his prophetic work on American democracy, but it has gained momentum during the past fifty years—the period during which the Ascent of Woman has taken place in America—and reached its climax in Riesman's other-directed Lonely Crowd.

The American woman and the Italian woman are so different, they seem to belong to two different species.

Of course they started from different premises; as long ago as 1840, an American traveler in Italy, J. T. Headley, noticed the difference.

Morally, the American appeared preferable to that observer. "I will not speak of moral qualities. For here the 'dark-eyed beauty' of Italy must lose in comparison; and indeed, with all her passionate nature, she is not capable of so lasting affection as an American. She is fiercer, wilder, but more changeable." Physically, aethetically, however, the Italian seemed superior. "In form, the Italians excel us. Larger, fuller, they naturally

acquire a finer gait and bearing. It is astonishing that our ladies
should persist in that ridiculous notion that a small waist is, and
per necessita must be, beautiful. Why, many an Italian woman
would cry for vexation, if she possessed such a waist as some of
our ladies acquire, only by the longest, painfullest process."[7]

Headley noticed the gaiety, the gracefulness of the Italian
women; "Your Italian knows how to laugh, and by the way, she
knows how to walk, which an American lady does not. An
American walks better than an Englishwoman, who steps like a
grenadier, but still she walks badly. Her movements lack grace,
ease, and naturalness."

He also noticed the sensual responsiveness of the Italian
woman, in contrast with the frigid Puritanism and the haughti-
ness of the American, who takes for granted all that comes to
her. "There is no country in the world, where woman is so
worshipped, and allowed to have her own way as in America,
and yet there is no country where she is so ungrateful for the
place and power she occupies."

Headley's discovery of the extraordinary power of the American woman as early as 1840 is as surprising as Tocqueville's
discovery of American mass culture about the same time. No
one in his senses, of course, would have connected woman's
power and collectivism in Tocqueville's time and Headley's.
Woman's power was rooted in quite different and quite peculiar
circumstances. It was rooted in the paucity of women in an immigrant population, and in the hard pioneer work, men's work,
accomplished by those relatively few women who settled the
country.

The harder the conditions of life, indeed, the sooner came
the emancipation of women. Wyoming adopted suffrage for
women as early as 1868, while it was still a territory, and insisted on this innovation when it acquired statehood twenty

years later. And it is no casual coincidence that in the pioneering West, feminism gained together with Populism.

By 1900:

... wives might own and control their separate property in three-fourths of the states; in every state a married woman might dispose, by will, of her separate property; in about two-thirds of the states she possessed her earnings; in the great majority she might make contracts and bring suit. In many states the law provided that if the wife engaged in business by herself or went outside the home to work, her earnings were her own, but all the fruits of her labor within the household still belonged to her husband. Fathers and mothers had equal guardianship of children in nine states.[8]

As the nineteenth century drew to a close, the United States was still a prevalently rural community. "Two-thirds of the nation's population still lived in rural areas in 1890, and nearly half of its families still made their living from the soil."[9]

But by that time, urbanization and industrialization took on momentum, and were soon to gain the upper hand. Between 1880 and 1890, New York City grew from a million to a million and a half people, and both Philadelphia and Chicago passed the million mark.

It is impossible to say how far the frontier elevation of women would have gone, or how successful would have been the noble efforts of the Women's Rights Convention of Seneca Falls, and the subsequent agitation of famous fighters like Lucretia Mott, Elizabeth Stanton, Lucy Stone and Susan Anthony, had they not all been engulfed by the movement from farm to city to megalopolis; by the development of industry to mass production.

The number of working women had been growing throughout the course of American history, but the rate of growth had been slow. As recently as 1940, six out of seven married women were housewives, and nothing else. However, since the beginning of the Second World War, the rate has notably accelerated.

By 1960, one-third of all married women, and more than half of all women between the ages of eighteen and fifty-five, were working, full-time or part-time, outside the home; the number is still rising. Women, thus, constitute 33 per cent of the total labor force. They are factory workers: in the garment, textile, tobacco, and other nondurable goods industries; 6.8 million women are office workers: file clerks, office-machine operators, typists, stenographers, secretaries; another 3.5 million are "service workers": waitresses, cooks, beauticians, manicurists, etc.; another 1.5 million are busy as salesgirls and in other commercial transactions. There are .5 million registered and student nurses, and 1,334,000 women teachers. About three-fourths of all teachers below college level are women; of college and university professors, one-fifth are women.

Yes, the American women seem to belong to a different species than the Italian.

Attention: Pan American Airways is announcing the departure of jet flight 417 to Karachi at Gate 5. Will passengers please get ready to board the aircraft?

It is a hot day. The Smiths get up from their lounge chairs in the waiting room. Mrs. Smith, in her light cotton dress, looks as though she were going to take a half-hour ride to the seashore. Joannie, who is nine, with a proud pony tail, takes her toddling brothers by their hands, one left, one right. The little boys, in T shirts and overalls, are replete with holsters and pistols and big cowboy hats. Each child carries his blue PAA overnight bag. Mr. Smith, in a seersucker suit, has the cameras, a brief case, and two suitcases, while Mrs. Smith carries the baby in a portable plastic crib. She looks as slim and trim as though she were the children's older sister. The baby wears nothing but a cotton shirt and a diaper. His round rosy legs are kicking lustily in the open air.

Mr. Smith is a foreign service man who has been transferred

from Rome to Karachi. His Italian friends, who have come to
see the family off, are leaning on the railing, waving, wondering.

"What courage, that woman," Signora Rossi says, "to travel
by plane with four small children, and no nurse." No Italian
woman would travel around half the world with four small
children unless she had at least one nursemaid to take along.
Besides, Italian women who belong to the Smiths' bracket and
could afford a nursemaid on a trip like this, very rarely have
four small children. And, if they do have four children, they do
not look like their children's older sister; they are matrons, heavy
and tired and nervous.

Yesterday the Smiths had their farewell party. There were
about fifty guests. The turkey, which Mrs. Smith had roasted
herself, and the ham which she had baked, were delicious. "And
here we had thought American women served everything out of
cans," the Italian ladies said, full of admiration. "I don't see
how you do it, what with the departure tomorrow," they said.

The trunks, of course, had left a month before, so there was
really not much to do.

That morning, Mrs. Smith had been to the gallery to super-
vise the crating of her paintings. Mrs. Smith is quite a good
painter, and just before leaving she had been invited to organize
a personal show—which she had done. It had been very successful. Now the paintings had to be shipped back to New York.

The day before, Mrs. Smith wound up her classes at the
American school. They had been short of teachers there, and
she had been helping out three times a week.

The other days she attended lessons in art history, because
sooner or later she expects to take her Ph.D. in this field, and
the years in Italy had offered a precious opportunity for studying.

Also, of course, she ran the Church committee, she organized the rummage sale, and bravely carried all the other responsibilities that fall on a foreign service wife's shoulders.

To us, all this seems perfectly natural. But the Italian ladies keep shaking their heads as they wave good-by to the departing Smiths. An upper-class woman who gets up at seven, takes no nap after lunch, has no headaches, no "nerves," and holds together motherhood, social obligations, and a professional life of her own, a wife and mother who studies for a university degree —all this is totally inconceivable to the Italian woman. She collapses at the mere thought of the amount of energy and work involved in this sort of life.

The American woman lives in a different moment of feminine evolution, of social evolution; therefore, she is different, psychologically and physically.

Neither the changes in the social structure nor the changes in the nature of woman were "planned," however. Evolution proceeded through a series of random mutations, not according to an over-all scheme. Random mutations mean trials and errors, progressions and regressions. Hence, the continued uncertainty as to the scope of women's education, evidenced in such recent, up-to-date, and intelligent studies as Mueller's *Educating Women for A Changing World,*[10] or Stoddard's *On the Education of Women.*[11] Mirra Komarovsky, in *Women in the Modern World,*[12] speaks of a "neo-antifeminist attack on women's colleges," summed up in the letter of one college woman, who complains: "I have come to realize that I was educated to be a successful man, and now must learn by myself how to be a successful woman."

Compared to Italian standards, the standards of American women's education are very high, reflecting the more advanced point reached in their evolution. According to a recent survey by the National Science Foundation, women currently earn about one-third of all bachelors' and masters' degrees. But this is as far as they go. Only about ten per cent of all doctorates go to women. Other—more collectivist—countries are much farther ahead, as we shall see.

The remedies proposed to recuperate lost feminine talent— by instituting part-time and adult-education courses and scholarships for women to reactivate and complete their studies after the completion of the child-bearing and -rearing phase of their lives—can only be partially successful. They may swell the lower ranks of women technicians, doctors, scientists. They hardly will catapult many women to the top ranks of genius. Genius is a full-time job, jealously exacting a lifetime of dedication. Men know that. Women who still consider homemaking their first and "natural" vocation are out. There is no way of getting around it.

In upholding the states' right to excuse—or even exclude— women from jury duty, Supreme Court Justice Harlan recently said:

Despite the enlightened emancipation of women from the restrictions and protections of bygone years, and their entry into many parts of community life formerly considered to be reserved to men, woman is still regarded as the center of home and family life. The lifting of such restrictions and protections as might jeopardize this position in the center of home and family, therefore, cannot be considered as imposed by the Constitution, and is not advisable.

As could have been expected, the Court's "progressive wing"— Justices Warren, Black, and Douglas—did not concur in the majority opinion which thus sanctioned the right of Alabama, Mississippi, and South Carolina to prohibit women from serving on juries.

Thus, basically, the American Supreme Court is divided, as had been, a few weeks earlier, the Italian Supreme Court, with regard to the equal rights of men and women's position in society. Even in America, double standards are still applied on a number of issues. Men are drafted, women are not. Until a few years ago, the idea of drafting women would have sounded absurd—something out of Plato or Campanella—but today, countries, such as Israel, exist where women are drafted just as are men. There is really no reason why they should not be. The law holds, in most states, that divorcing women may sue men for alimony; divorcing men may not. And yet, if a woman's work is worth a man's, there should be no difference. As long as women do not have the same duties as men—and in a modern society there is no reason why they should not—their rights are bound to remain sham, at least to some extent.

Thus there is uncertainty. The feminine and masculine mind continue to be tested, analyzed, catalogued. Statistics are piling up. Yet woman's place in society, the real scope of her life, her hierarchy of values, remain undefined. Doubts, as always, are accompanied by pangs of conscience. The family is disintegrating. Juvenile delinquency is on the increase. And how many people still lay the blame on the working mother's doorstep! In *Sex and Morality,* for instance, Abram Kardiner asserts that "children reared on a spare-time basis will show the effects of such care in the disturbances of character that inevitably result. Motherhood is a full-time job."[13] The total absence of juvenile delinquency in the Israeli *kibbutzim*—where *all* mothers work— would seem to belie this assertion.

Margaret Mead states in *Male and Female,* "We end up with the contradictory picture of a society that appears to throw the doors wide open to women, but translates her every step toward success as having been damaging"[14]—to her own chances, to her children, and to men. Everyone is frustrated, everyone is alienated, and all together, they make up a lonely crowd.

On close examination, the American scene presents all these aspects. But looking at it from a distance, one realizes that, by trial and error, and with the penalties this process entails, there has emerged a society whose collectivism represents—or represented, until a few years ago—the most advanced form of social evolution. And with it has emerged a type of woman whose physical and mental structure is more evolved—or was until a few years ago—than other woman's, anywhere else.

According to the predictions of the U. S. Bureau of Labor Statistics, 13.5 million more workers will be needed in 1970 than were needed in 1960. Almost half of the additional workers will be women, which makes a twenty-five per cent increase for women workers, as against a fifteen per cent increase for men.

Nine out of ten young women will join the labor force, which brings us close to the pattern of social economy of the communist world. Obviously this will require further changes in the psychology of the American woman.

NINE

Ascent of Woman
Cruising Altitude

Women can get ahead more easily in underdeveloped countries. I feel that in India and Ceylon, for example, women come forward at about the same time that men do, and are taken more for granted than in the nations where women traditionally take a back seat to men. These women have missed the repressive Victorian Era, and skipping the nineteenth century can be helpful.

ALVA MYRDAL[1]

We have invited Tommaso Campanella and Thomas More to join us on our airplane flight. We are flying low, you remember. We are flying over Israel now.

"Look," Campanella says, "the City of the Sun."

We are flying over a new *kibbutz,* a co-operative village. Cultivated fields, alternating with rectangles of wooded land, fan out regularly from a perfectly round urbanistic structure: a belt of white pavilions with pink roofs, orchards and greenery, cut at even distances by roads leading like rays from the center to the outside. Inside, a ringlike avenue, enclosing more green and amply laid-out public buildings. It is a harmonious, calm, pleasing sight: and in its perfect roundness and with its rays, it does look like the City of the Sun.

As we land we notice in the distance, a long line of soldiers approaching us. We wait.

Heavy boots. Three-quarter-length wide breeches. Open, belted shirts. Some wear steel helmets, some wear caps. Heavy baggage. Machine guns. Here are two with automatic rifles under their arms. Their caps are stuck in their belts. They have black, flowing hair; dark, almond-shaped eyes; no make-up on their pretty, open faces. These soldiers, returning from a day of maneuvering, are all women. "You see," Campanella insists, "we have landed in the City of the Sun."

From the left, another column of soldiers is drawing closer. They are *Guades,* just drafted. Here boys and girls in identical uniforms march side by side.[2]

183

We turn to the lieutenant, a girl of about twenty-two. Straight posture. There is authority and earnestness in her expression, but there is nothing unfeminine. She has some of the melancholy of her people. She sees far though she is young. Her cap is rakishly aslant on her black head of hair. She is cordial. She is hospitable.

"Girls are drafted just like boys in Israel, of course," she explains. "If women have the same rights, they have to have the same duties. We do office work, yes, and hospital work. But we are trained for combat, too. Serious work. The night maneuvers; and the marching. A hundred miles through the desert, with heavy arms and baggage. Sixty pounds of it. Sometimes the girls don't know how to carry on. At night, almost dead, we collapse in our tents. We sleep on the ground, fully dressed. No use crying. Tomorrow we go on marching."[3]

Campanella is squirming. This goes even farther than he had hoped for. This is no "stationary work" these girls are doing. They each carry a man's burden.

"But the army is really wonderful," the lieutenant continues. "My parents came from the States. I could have gone to college there. But I prefer the army. It's a college for the people. For rich and poor, from all nations. We study. And we learn to live and to belong. Not only to fight, but to build. To use tractors, not only machine guns. We work in the fields, we found new *kibbutzim*. And when we are through with our military training, we just stay there."

Here the sword is being beaten into a plowshare.

"The City of the Sun," Campanella repeats.

"For two years," Thomas More remembers, "they have to join, together with the men, the labor draft, in charge of the nation's agriculture. For husbandry is a science in common to all in general, both men and women, wherein they all be expert and cunning."

We enter the village. The first thing we notice is the Children's House: a modern building, clean, white, with flowers everywhere—there are flowers in front of all the houses. Inside are nurseries, dormitories large and small, classrooms with the most modern equipment, friendly dining rooms with tables and chairs in all sizes, workshops, play rooms, gyms. "Here," we are told by an energetic housemother in a white apron smock who has come to greet us, "the children of the entire community are raised. Here they sleep, eat, study, play, and work."

She shows us the neat bedrooms of the older children. Each room houses four youngsters—two boys and two girls—up to the age of eighteen. Campanella can't help chuckling. After all, he is an Italian. Just think what would happen in Italy if you assigned common bedrooms to boys and girls that age. . . . But here they have been raised like brothers and sisters. Here they are equals, and the common dorms express and emphasize this absolute equality.

The children go home for three hours after work every evening, and on weekends and holy days. So the parents can work. So the private household is reduced to its bare essentials. So mothers can sleep at night, quietly, without crying babies.

Thomas More surmises that we really must be in Utopia. This was exactly the kind of children's house he had in mind.

His conviction, that it is indeed Utopia where we are, is confirmed when he sees the communal kitchen where the women are preparing a healthy and pleasurable meal for the whole community. "For it were a folly to take the pain to dress a bad dinner at home, when they may be welcome to good and fine fare so nigh hand at the hall," he says approvingly.

The hall, incidentally, is wonderfully built, equipped with the latest in sound-absorbing floors and walls. The large windows are hung with cheerful curtains. The furniture, made by the *kibbutzniks* themselves, is simple, modern, and tasteful. Modern paintings, some by famous artists, some by members of the *kibbutz,* adorn the walls.

"We have been fortunate," explains the woman whose turn it is to preside over the dining-room work. "Many of our members came from Germany; they have received large sums from the German government as *Wiedergutmachung,* indemnity. So we could afford the luxury of this community hall."

"Did they put all the money at the disposal of the *kibbutz?*" we ask, a bit naïvely.

"There is no such thing as private property among us," the woman answers severely. "Everybody works according to his capacity and receives according to his need: housing, food, clothing, a stipend to study at the university, medical care, tools; all we have we have in common. And we have much."

"The whole *kibbutz* ideology is based on the principle of absolute equality between men and women,"* the woman insists, a little later.

Our flight companions are simply delighted at seeing the women at work side by side with the men. We see them plow and sow, irrigate and reap, always a gun or pistol within arm's reach, in an atmosphere not unlike that of the old West—like the cowgirl, near the frontier, on her lean horse, with an ever-ready rifle slung over her shoulder. We see them handling machines, plying the arts and crafts. They take their full share in the cultural life of the community—the library, the orchestra, the theater and folk dancing; we see them participate in the spiritual life: the blue-eyed girl with long blond hair flowing over her white tunic, reading the Passover story at *Kibbutz Shefaim,*

---

* This, of course, is true to a large extent of any form of collective farming: of the Mexican *ejido,* as of the Russian *kolkhoz.* In all forms of collective farming, Henrik Infield points out in *Utopia and Experiment,* "the position of women becomes more nearly equal to that of man."[4] The more collectivist the form of farming, the more nearly equal is this position.

looks like a seventeenth-century Italian painting. Yet she works like a man and is to be drafted into the army next year.

We have been lucky, of course. The *kibbutz* we are visiting is a flourishing one. The reward has been commensurate to the aspiration, and all goes well.

Thomas More was quite put out when, visiting an older, poorer *kibbutz,* he received, instead of an answer, an outburst of screams and curses from a woman assigned to the kitchen work there. "She should be chastised by her husband," he mumbled. With time, disillusionment had come to this *kibbutz,* and with disillusionment, bitterness. The forms of collectivism were still there, but the forms had become empty. The faith was gone. People had begun to cheat. With the failure of collectivism, the "women's problem" had reared its ugly head.[5] A caste system had been developing, creating a managerial class in contrast to the common workers, and the more highly valued sector of productive work fell more and more into the hands of men, while women's activities were limited to services—children, cooking, cleaning, laundering—"feminine work," in other words. Demoted from her original status of equality—in the formative stage, women represented the most active and integrating element in the *kibbutz*—the women rebelled. They wanted pretty clothes now, they wanted privacy. They wanted their husbands and their children to themselves. They wanted a lot of things that were very real to them but are no longer real to the new *Sabra* generation. They tried to instigate an exodus from the *kibbutz.*

In short, some failed, other succeeded, but the *kibbutz* remains a remarkable and highly influential experiment in social organization.

Under various, converging influences, collectivism has reached a high point of intensity in this sector of Israeli life. Some of these influences were idealistic: the Tolstoyan-communist faith of immigrants from Eastern Europe. Some of them were material: the hardships of colonizing, the pressure coming from a hostile, belligerent Arab population. But the greatest influence of all was the need to create bonds, unifying bonds, among people who came from so many countries, from so many continents, and had so little in common.

The *kibbutz* and the army, one might say, are the most characteristic expressions of Israel's peculiar collectivism, and it is in both that we find the Ascent of Woman at its highest. The type of young woman that has emerged here among the *Sabra*—the generation born in Israel, especially in the *kibbutz*—is undoubtedly more modern, more evolved, than the American woman.

Lydia X., for example, a biology student at the Hebrew University, who has just finished her military service, knows nothing about a "woman's problem." She is about to marry a fellow student, and the total equality between the two is taken for granted, by them and by their environment. To make a home, to raise a family, are tasks incumbent on both, which do not interfere with their intellectual and professional lives. Both man and woman dedicate themselves, body and soul, to the construction of their new State, and the State, the community, the "collective," in turn, helps them with its social services in all their many forms. There is not even a question about that. How different from the American woman, with her doubts and fears!

The same forces we have seen at work in shaping the intense collectivism of the *kibbutzim* are at work in shaping a new kind of co-operative collectivism in the State of Israel as a whole: a social-democratic structure, of which the *kibbutz* collective constitutes such a large sector and such an important symbol. To gauge the influence of the *kibbutz* spirit on the nation as a whole, it is enough to remember that 250,000 Jews, of a total of two million, have passed through *kibbutzim;* that today the *kibbutzim* cultivate forty-one per cent of all cultivated areas; that over thirty per cent of the Ministers and twenty-five per cent of the members of Parliament come from *kibbutzim;* which, furthermore, furnish the elite of trade union and military personnel. Logically, the nation as a whole has developed, under this influence, a brand of collectivism reflected most obviously in its economic structure: soil, sub-soil, energy, means of transportation are all state-owned. A large part of the nation's industries is owned by the trade unions, seventy per cent of the land is cultivated co-operatively, and seventy-five per cent of the agricultural produce is marketed co-operatively.[6]

Thus, the absolute equality of men and women is a basic tenet of the State as a whole.

How high-powered the Ascent of Woman has been—during the brief span of one decade!—can be measured by the enormity of some of the obstacles that had to be overcome.

First of all, this new form of collectivism, implying the emancipation of woman and her full participation in the social and economic process, had to be grafted onto the religion of the patriarchs! Small wonder if it has been opposed within the ranks of the State itself, and if some people thought to discern some sort of incongruity between the old ideals and the new reality. Agudat Israel, with its workers' party, Poalei, keeps demanding the strict observance of the Torah in the administration of the State, the transfer of the State's juridical power to the rabbinate, and the abolition of the equality between men and women. The rabbinical courts, in fact, do not recognize the equality of women. According to rabbinical law, a man may divorce his wife, but a wife may not ask to divorce her husband, even when he has abandoned his family. Custody of the sons of a separated couple is entrusted to the father. Women are not recognized as witnesses in rabbinical courts.

Although Agudat is a small party, it is not totally without

influence, having on its side, if not right, at least some logic.

But more important, look at the raw material the State of
Israel has to build its modern structure! Consider the wild-
bearded men from Yemen, who, as L. F. Rushbrook Williams
vividly describes in *The State of Israel*,[7] confidently boarded the
Israeli plane that was to take them to the Holy Land because,
according to a prophecy of the sacred scriptures, they would
return to the land of their fathers on eagle's wings! When the
plane was evenly cruising at an altitude of fifteen thousand feet,
they happily hopped about into the aisles, then hovered in a
huddle toward the rear end to build a fire to cook their meal!

The dark, proud, shy women they brought with them were
good at painting pottery, at folk dancing—remember the magnificent prenuptial gowns of the girls—and at smoking water
pipes. At home, a woman is important, the men from Yemen
explained. But outside the home? Even men did not count much.
But a woman?

To think that families of this sort, from Yemen, Iraq, Lybia,
Morocco, Algeria, Tunisia, and other countries in Asia and
Africa, now make up almost sixty per cent of Israel's population, is enough to make one realize the enormity of the job
ahead: the absorption, the assimilation of these masses into a
modern state.

If the United States is a melting pot, with the group-force
action that this implies, Israel, it has been said, is a pressure
cooker—with the group-force intensified accordingly.

It may be considered fortunate that this Afro-Asian Jewish
population is, on the whole, a *young* population—in contrast to
the European Jewish population, which is aging. While the
education of the older generation may be doomed to partial
failure—the most to be hoped for from these older immigrants
being co-operation with the State in the education of the young
—the younger generation may well be assimilated in the course

of another ten to fifteen years. This is likely, considering the efficiency of a rapidly expanding network of kindergartens, schools, and social services, and the leveling, unifying influence of the military service.

Another factor which works in favor of the success of modern, collectivist Israel is a curious one that we shall have occasion to examine again later : it seems to be easier for a population to pass from a situation of pre-individual collectivism (like that of the clan-bound Yemen Jews) to a situation of post-individual collectivism (like that of modern Israel) than to get there from a situation of individualism.

This would be, it seems to us, in more generalized terms, the meaning of Alva Myrdal's statement quoted at the head of this chapter. This is the explanation, too, of a recent observation of Mrs. Pandit. "The strange thing," she said to an interviewer of the New York *Herald Tribune* (September 3, 1961), "is that the countries of the East have given women equality whereas the far more socially advanced countries of the West still suspect their women. I think there is no question," she added, "but that as time goes on, even the slow moving West will catch up with us and give women more places of responsibility."

Under unique pressures and influences, a new type of collectivism is thus being forged in Israel, and with it, a new type of modern woman : free, and man's equal. One of this new type is the Minister of Foreign Affairs, the indefatigable Golda Meir, mighty in council; another is so outstanding a scientist as Professor Rosin of the Cancer Research Project of the Medical Faculty of the Hebrew University, the face of a prophet. The new bridge over the Yarken River, just beyond Tel Aviv, was planned and built by a woman. The chief chemist of the Bureau of Standards, responsible for the quality of Israel's consumer goods, is a woman. The head of the Haifa Technion's Building Research Station is a woman professor of civil engineering who was recently elected president of the International Union of Testing and Research Laboratories for Structures.

At the Hebrew University's 1959 commencement, ten of sixty-two doctorates in the natural sciences went to women; fourteen of sixty-six degrees in medicine; thirteen of twenty-two masters' degrees in bacteriology; as well as almost half of the one hundred twenty baccalaureates in the humanities.[8] Almost two-thirds of the country's primary and secondary school teachers are women; and most of the teachers in the army—for both men and women—are women, corporals or sergeants; for, according to Israeli experience, "women get far better results as teachers for adults than men. Far better."[9]

Women constitute about ten per cent of the members of Parliament and twenty-three per cent of the total labor force. With the coming of age of the new generation, this trend is continually and rapidly expanding. These women soldiers, students, and workers, show to a high degree what Melford Spiro postulates in his book *Kibbutz:* "Identification with the group, a sense of security within the group, an absence of intense acquisitive drives, the absence of intense success strivings, a willingness to assume social responsibilities."[10] These are the characteristics of a highly evolved type of woman.

The U.S.S.R. In 1928, women industrial workers and salaried employees in the Soviet Union numbered 1,284,000. In 1958 their number had risen to 12,650,000! In agriculture, women workers and employees rose from 416,000 to 2,006,000 during the same period. At the outbreak of World War II, there were 250,000 women chiefs of tractor brigades, 350,000 women chiefs of cattle-raising squadrons and brigades, and 15,000 women were elected as chairmen of *kolkhoz* administrations.

In 1917, Russia counted 600 women engineers; by 1948 their number had risen to 250,000, by 1958 to 293,300, constituting almost 30 per cent of the total number of engineers in the Soviet Union. Well over 3,000,000 women work in the sector of public education. Over 2,500,000 women are employed in public health; 110,500 women are economists, statisticians, and merchandizing specialists, constituting 60 per cent of the total personnel in this field.

In politics, over 500,000 women belong to the direction of local soviets, from the periphery to the center; 348 women are deputies to the Supreme Soviet, constituting almost 26 per cent of its total membership. Eight women belong to the Central Executive Committee of the Communist Party (which has 133 members). Twenty thousand village soviets are headed by women.

Of all Soviet citizens who have acquired diplomas or Ph.D.s in institutions of higher learning or universities since the Soviet government took over, 42.3 per cent are women. In the United States, as we have seen, the total is about 20 per cent, if we add bachelors' and masters' degrees to the Ph.D.s. Thirty-six per cent of all Soviet scientific research workers are women.

It has been pointed out repeatedly in recent years that the nearer we get to the summit of Soviet power, the scarcer women become.

Down, way down, you can see squads of women street sweepers, with big white aprons over their heavy clothes, scarves on their heads, their palms calloused from handling those big brooms eight hours a day, six days a week. That's no job for a woman.

Here, they are building a new palace; two-thirds of the brick-layers are women. There, they are mixing mountains of cement, hauling heavy pails. At the street corner, the traffic is being diverted. They are digging a hole for the underground pipelines. Twelve feet below ground, gray forms are moving about, shoveling earth. Clumsy, in quilted coats, their legs stuck in heavy felt boots with rubber galoshes over them, were it not for the kerchiefs wrapping their heads, you would have no way to recognize these as women.

A siren is sounding; there, a column of workers is directed toward the steel mill. About half of them are women—stocky, heavy, broad-faced women, in slacks, in blue or gray or black sweaters.

You call that *Ascent of Woman*? I'd call it *descent,* the critics say.

Descent, ascent. The earth is round, and if we move away from it, who can tell whether we are ascending or descending? What we mean by the Ascent of Woman—let us be prudent—is her rapid movement away from a center thus far thought to be solid.

In the higher echelons, yes, there are women, the critics say, but few in proportion to men. There should be more. And at the top there has never been one.

Professor Nicholas DeWitt points out in *Educational Professional Employment in the USSR:*

The proportion of "leading personnel" positions held by women varied significantly from field to field. Thus in industry and construction women occupied only thirty-one and twenty-two per cent, respectively, of the "leading personnel" jobs. In education and cultural services and in public health, however, women represented sixty-six and eighty-eight per cent, respectively, of the "leading personnel."

If the proportion of women in the "leading personnel" category is compared with the proportion of women among all workers and employees, it becomes apparent that in all branches and sectors of the Soviet economy, except public health and research and development, the proportion of women in the workers and employees category is considerably higher than the proportion of women employed as leading administrative, managerial and specialized personnel. Clearly, while Soviet women have made major advancements into leading positions, they do not yet occupy these jobs in numbers proportionate to their participation in total employment.[11]

The Soviet policy of total and absolute legal equality of men and women and its implementation with nurseries, kindergartens, community kitchens, and so forth, has helped the emancipation of women; but it has not been enough to solve the "women's problem." A housewife, a mother, has her handicaps in Russia, too—else she should have risen to the top ranks by now. Uncertainty and involution have existed in Russia, too.

The number of kindergartens is steadily and rapidly growing. In 1961, 1,288,000 babies were taken care of in crèches, and there were 47,000 kindergartens accommodating 3,000,000 preschool children. To these institutions, which function all the year round, should be added about 38,000 camps for children of various ages.

These are respectable numbers.

Yet, a Soviet propaganda pamphlet of a few years ago proudly stated that "the majority of children, however, are still raised in the bosom of the family, under the loving care of the mothers, grandmothers, and aunts."[12]

But a loving mother who has to wash swaddling clothes—in Russia, babies are still swaddled as of old, board-stiff, up to the age of nine months; which, according to the British anthropologist Geoffrey Gorer, has a lasting effect on the Russian character—and who has to divide her loving care between job and children, is as handicapped in her ascent in Russia as anywhere else.

The Stalin era was an era of involution with regard to the family as in every other regard. There is no question about that. Even the principle of coeducation was questioned under Stalin. "Today [in 1950] in seventy major towns and cities where the schools are very large, there is separate education. In all other schools, coeducation remains," the delegates of the International Union of Students reported. "However, there is a great interest in the results of the different systems, and it is believed that in certain cases, separate education is preferable because of the different rates of biological development and the different characteristics of boys and girls."[13] These different characteristics, if stressed from early childhood on, of course increase with development—and thus, we are back to the "biological tragedy of woman," which accounts for her failure in making good, even if given equal chances with men! A failure that would be the more tragic because the equal chances, elsewhere merely talked about, had really been made concrete here.

But let us be fair. Let us look again at the figures. In spite of the involution of the Stalin era, women's gainful employment was at its highest point in 1950, when they constituted forty-seven per cent of the total labor force. This is an impressive figure, which can be explained partly—but only partly—by the shortage of manpower due to war casualties. The number of women, in certain age groups, was crushingly superior to the number of men in the years immediately after the war. Among people aged thirty-five, there were, according to John Gunther, seven women for every one man. Evidently this disequilibrium in the sex ratio accounts for a part of the great number of women workers in an ever-growing number of sectors. We should remember, however, that the rate of growth of the number of women workers was even faster in the decade 1930–40— without war—than in the decade 1940–50; presumably, this development would have continued if there had been no war.

Professor DeWitt points out that the depletion of male manpower "had already begun to occur during the 1930's, when forced collectivization and a reign of terror [purges and concentration camps] caused heavy, multi-million losses, among the male population especially."[14] He does not say anything more

specific about this differential death rate. But let us assume that
it was very high. Many are the ways of the Lord; and of the
Devil; and of Statistics, the new goddess of fate. The fact
remains that the pre-eminence of women—perhaps even their
numerical superiority—is connected with an intense drive toward
collectivization, both in industry and agriculture.

Between 1950 and 1955 there was a drop of two per cent in
the female labor force, due to the maturing of a generation with
a more even sex ratio. In 1955, women made up forty-five per
cent of the total labor force, but since then they have regained
one per cent.

Within this enormous reservoir of womanpower, however,
some shifts have taken place which, although slight up to this
day, may nevertheless signify a new trend. If this trend were
confirmed and intensified during the coming years, the U.S.S.R.
would appear like a giant *kibbutz*—one of those older ones,
where a flagging of the collectivist spirit of the pioneers had
entailed a re-shift of female labor from productive work to the
"services." There has been a noticeable drop in the percentage
of women workers in industry, building and construction, ma-
chine-tractor stations, and agriculture in general. The service
sectors, on the other hand, show a sharp rise. According to the
most recent statistics presented by DeWitt, the women employed
in National Economy, Production, Distribution, and Management constitute forty-two per cent of the total labor force employed in these branches; the women employed in the Social
Services constitute seventy-six per cent.

As for the decrease in the productive sectors, the Russian
authorities themselves have been somewhat apologetic all along
for the heavy load of work of their women bricklayers, plumbers, crane operators, welders. The future will lighten this burden, they say.

If they mean that heavy manual work is going to be abolished both for men and women because it is going to be mechanized, they are undoubtedly on the right track of economic evolution. If they mean that, as long as heavy manual work exists, it is preferable that it be done by men and that it is unseemly for a woman to do a man's work, they may well be on the wrong track.*

Heavy work did not harm the health of the primitive women of pre-individual societies. It does not seem to harm the sturdy women of post-individual society. To be quite honest, these Russian bricklayers, plumbers and welders look a lot healthier than the bloodless middle-class ladies in more individualistic societies—who do nothing at all.

He who wants to be a good pope must know how to be a good sacristan, an Italian proverb says. He, or she, who wants to reach the top ranks, must be able to serve in the lowest.

The progress of mechanization and automation tends to equalize the work of men and women. In a totally mechanized economic system, women can do, and do do, all the jobs men can do. If, in the Soviet society, there are still jobs that must be done by men rather than by women, or vice versa, it simply means that the Ascent of Woman is not yet totally realized.

But the shift, during these last years, from productive work to the services—"stationary work," Campanella would say—in the feminine labor force is very slight, indeed, affecting less than ten per cent of womanpower. Too soon to cry "failure!" During the same period, the percentage of women among Soviet professionals has been steadily going up. And even if they are not yet one-hundred per cent successful, the women in this totalitarian-collectivist society have reached a measure of elevation far

---

* In the 1870's, when the typewriter made its first appearance in American business, women were considered unsuitable as operators. "Their capacities to stand the physical strain of operating such machines was seriously questioned by concerned citizens."[15]

above that reached in any other society—except one, to which we shall refer later.

The charts and maps spread out before us as we fly over the Soviet Union all show one high point of feminine achievement. Its existence has been attested to by everyone in a most matter-of-fact way, whereas no one—strangely enough—has taken the trouble to explore, to explain it. This high point is medicine. Let us draw closer.

The study of medicine is hard and long. Few are the girls in the Western countries who have the stamina to stick it out. The study of anatomy, the dissection of corpses, can be disturbing even to boys, let alone girls. The practicing physician has a hard life. Though he earns well, his privacy is often invaded, even during the night. He must be ever-ready for emergency calls. The surgeon, on his feet eight hours a day, with steady hand and imperturbable mind and nerves, is strictly a masculine figure in the Western world. The few exceptions seem only to confirm the rule.

In the Soviet Union, 75.5 per cent of all doctors and surgeons are women!

Since the Revolution, the total number of physicians has multiplied seventeen times. The number of women doctors has grown one-hundred-twenty-five-fold! This development is unique in the world and really astonishing. What is the explanation?

"It is believed that women have a particular aptitude for medical studies," a booklet of the International Union of Students laconically suggests.[16]

But why should they have this particular aptitude in Russia when they do not have it in Italy or in the United States? Or, if they have it universally, why should it have been up to the Soviet Union to discover it?

As far as we can see, the reasons are two, and interconnected.

In the early revolutionary days, the study of medicine was considered a symbol in the fight for the emancipation of women. In the 1870's the first Russian women graduated from the medical faculty of the University of Zurich—among them, Vera Figner, one of the great heroic figures of pre-revolutionary days. More than a profession or a personal career, medicine, for these socialist women, was a social service. When they returned to Russia, they settled in the countryside, among the disinherited and the poor, and made of their professional activity an effective vehicle for revolutionary propaganda. Many of them—like Vera Figner—suffered persecution, exile, or imprisonment.

Linking medicine, socialism, and the emancipation of women, these precursors set a pattern that kept acting on the professional choices of Soviet women, as well as on the evolution of Soviet medicine.

Soviet medicine, in fact, has become a gigantic social service, dedicated to an infinity of minor routine activities in prophylactics and hygiene and diet, prenatal and postnatal controls, the health of children at school, and others, which do not require the ministrations of a great doctor, but rather those of a well-trained nurse. Thus, a new type of medical officer has developed in the Soviet Union: the *feldsher* is a graduate, not from a university, but from a *tekhnikum*. There are about 3,700 of these institutions in the Soviet Union, giving two- and two-and-one-half-year courses to graduates of the ten-year schools. The *feldsher* thus occupies a place midway between a doctor and nurse. "And under a socialist state, isn't this obviously a good idea?" William Benton comments. "I assume that from fifty to ninety per cent of the average American medical practitioner's responsibilities could be readily handled by a *feldsher,* and just as competently,"[17] he concludes.

These *feldshers,* or social-service medical officers, are almost all women.

This does not mean that women in Soviet medicine are restricted to the *feldsher*-level. At the university-level medical school, almost eighty per cent of the students are women. Some of the U.S.S.R.'s most outstanding and hard-working surgeons are women. The hospital of Krakovo near Moscow, for instance, is directed by a woman surgeon, Alexandra Tchébotariova, a "Heroine of Soviet Labor," who has to her credit over ten thousand surgical operations! Women also abound in the top ranks of researchers, in cancer research, cardiology, gerontology, and the resuscitation of the "dead"—fields to which Soviet science has made outstanding contributions. The number of women doctors in the Soviet Union is, according to DeWitt, 285,400! In the United States, the American Medical Directory reported a total of 13,095 women physicians in 1958. According to the figures of the U. S. Census Bureau, this is 6.1 per cent of the total number of practicing physicians and surgeons.

The field of medicine thus offers a surprising confirmation of our thesis: socialization, collectivization, brings on, and is brought on by, the Ascent of Woman.*

In Communist China, post-individual collectivism, pushed ruthlessly further than anywhere else in the world, follows close on pre-individual collectivism—the phase of individualism, of middle-class emancipation, having died abortively after a brief gestation period of some thirty years.

Here the individual has never emerged from the crushing context of the "extended family," obedient ever, self-effacing ever. Unconditional subordination to the older generation, un-

---

* In England the number of women doctors has increased from ten thousand to twelve thousand since the socialization of medicine in 1948—a steady, if not spectacular, increase. Women now constitute twenty per cent of the whole medical profession in England.

flinching acceptance of his place in a stable hierarchy, have
bereft the Chinese through the millennia of the opportunity to
develop initiative and individuality. The Chinese household was,
as Koestler says of the Indian one, "a school of conformity,
obedience, resignation."[18] The ultimate goal of its education
was "the shedding of the ego, its passions, appetites, ambitions,
idiosyncracies: the elimination of individuality."

It is not surprising that human beings, raised in a collective
like the Chinese family, should want to re-establish these values
in the larger collective, the State, once the old order gave way
to the pressures of economic evolution and a shrinking world.

In *Brave New World Revisited,* Huxley is aghast at the
perfection of the Chinese Communist brainwashing methods:
the skill, employed in prisons and "re-education camps," with
which they wield the weeding hoes of threat and terror to uproot
individuality, and then proceed to reconstruct a different personality, gently planting and cultivating a new soul, a new mind,
a new memory, a new temperament—of strict Marxist-Stalinist
shape. But this is merely a bigger and better variety of what
Koestler, speaking of the traditional Japanese family, tenderly
calls "character gardening." "The invisible wire rack planted
into the nervous system" twists behavior into a stylized pattern,
"like the shape of the *bon-sai* tree, until it has become 'second
nature.' "

Science takes over where magic left off.

The step from pre-individualism to post-individualism is
short indeed, demographic and economic pressures concurring.

In 1939, when the average income per person was $554 in
the United States and $283 in France, it was $34 in India and
$29 in China! Everything else lagged in about the same propor-
tion. Consumption of energy per individual per day was seventy-
five times higher in the United States than in China. The United
States had constructed eighty thousand meters of rails per

thousand square miles; China, for the same area, three. The number of motorized cars in the United States was two hundred fifty per thousand inhabitants, in China, two-tenths per thousand. The food ration of the Chinese was about one-fifth of the Frenchman's, with an extremely low protein content. The average life span of Americans was sixty-four years; of the Chinese twenty-five.[19] With eighty-five per cent of the land uncultivated, its natural resources virtually untapped; without heavy industry; with a population ninety per cent illiterate, crushed by disease and famine—what was there to be done? Can we really be surprised if the remedy turned out to be as extreme as the evil, in that a form of collectivism developed the like of which the world has never seen?

But, "the road to collectivization is also that which grants to women a human dignity," writes Simone de Beauvoir. Collectivization means the Ascent of Woman.

Much has been written about the abject conditions of women in pre-Communist China: perhaps even too much, inasmuch as it often seems, by implication, that the lot of men must have been better. It hardly was. Civil liberties, the rights of the individual, were, of course, unknown both to men and women. Decisions always were made by others, by the older generations, both for men and women. Forced marriage, child marriage, inflicted unhappiness not only on the women. Child slave labor existed both for boys and girls, and hunger and toil and epidemic disease was the common lot of both.

The ancient Chinese had goddesses as well as gods, and powerful empresses who shrewdly governed for their minor sons. Ancestor worship included both males and females. Productive work—especially in southern China—made women an essential part of the community. The figure of the mother, or of the mother-in-law—still surviving in our days—is powerful and second only to that of the patriarch. Age was a stronger factor in determining the pecking order than was sex. The young man bowed to the old woman.

But the old, pre-individual collective was caving in, Mao or no Mao, giving way to the pressures of evolution; and when a collective order slackens, it is always the women who suffer most. Prostitution in China was flourishing if nothing else was.

The lower the point of departure, the more spectacular the ascent. The metamorphosis of Chinese women is the most exalting miracle in all Asia, exclaimed a Chinese, non-Communist, Catholic woman doctor, who lives near Singapore.

Mao conquered China with an army that contained women —"round faces," the Chinese call them—as well as men, to the astonishment of all.[20]

The Chinese Constitution provides, with a profusion of detail, for the total equality between men and women. Forced marriages, child marriages, polygamy, bigamy, are prohibited by law. Divorce is open to both men and women. Husband and wife have the same rights and the same duties, also, with regard to their children. They ought to love one another, respect one another, assist one another, to live in harmony, to share the burden of work and production, to raise their children, to share in the pursuit of happiness, and to collaborate in the construction of a new society (Article 8). Each one is free to choose his or her own profession. Each one keeps his or her name. In case of death, the surviving spouse inherits the possessions of the deceased (Articles 9–12).[21]

Girls have the same right to education as boys; much, however, remains to be done in this field. Due to the terrible shortage of schools and teachers, education has not yet been made compulsory either for boys or for girls. But already, 35 per cent of all primary school children, 31 per cent of all secondary school children, and 26 per cent of all university students, are girls.

Women have been allotted land, just like men. Forty per cent of Chinese women are employed as industrial workers. Women employees in public offices have quadrupled, occupying places ranging from the lowest to the highest. The number of women Deputies has been steadily rising: in 1957 they constituted 13 per cent of the legislature; in 1961, 22.5 per cent. The Ministers of Justice, of Foreign Affairs, of the Interior, of Public Health, at the moment of this writing, are all women. So is the Vice-President of the Republic, Mme. Sung Ch'ing-ling, daughter of Sun Yat-sen and sister of Nationalist China's first lady, Mme. Chiang Kai-shek.*

For only fifteen years of Communist reign, this, certainly, is a fantastic record.

Although the emancipation of women—together with that of men—is the acknowledged goal of the whole Afro-Asian liberation movement, and much, very much, is being done to make it a reality, no other country, not even India, not even Indonesia, has similar results to show. The struggle with tradition is a hard one, and even though individual women have risen to top positions, the masses are lagging behind, and the effort to get millions of women and girls to school has been so far only partially successful.[22]

Following the Ascent of Woman we have taken a bird's-eye view of her situation in five countries: in Western Europe, North America, the Middle East, Eastern Europe, and the Far East. We have taken off from a land where individualism is still strong, and the estate of woman low, though beginning to rise. What we could discern last was a continent of rabid collectivism, where women were being catapulted into positions of leadership and power.

Certainly, many ingredients have gone into the fuel powering this ascent. Some creating the preconditions for others, some

---

* The story of the hostile sisters at the head of the two factions of this great suffering nation in this period of transition, would make a fine subject for a modern Greek-style tragedy.

canceling others, some abetting others. But the mainspring of this ascent's energy is the collectivist drive: from pre-individualism to post-individualism; through individualism or without it.

Our way of piloting has been rather ruthless at times; and we shall be accused of superficiality, lack of precision, disregard for innumerable details that would not fit our scheme. We have tried to move in a modern spirit of synthesis, away from the trend toward specialization that characterized the scholarly work of the nineteenth century. This is always dangerous, and we are waiting for the radar of the specialists, down there on earth, to catch up with us—and for their missiles to tear us to pieces—if they think it worth-while to do so.

We are flying very high now. Time has shrunk, and we see the earthball as from a sputnik. Just look: *This is the age of the peopling of the earth. The growth during one century has been greater than during all the previous ages.*[23] Growing numbers. Growing numbers. Growing numbers. We are so far away that we can see mankind in its wider biological context. We see that growing numbers, interacting with an indeterminate number of indeterminate factors, produce a yet greater group-force and a growing amount of femininity. We are far enough away to disregard details. Look! Europe is lighter in growing numbers. North America and Russia show the darker color of faster increase, and China is almost black with growing numbers of people.

So far away are we that this earthball appears to us as a single free-floating hive, covered all over with swarming, buzzing human beings.

Still rising, we see all the humans-bees-cells join into one new super-organism that wants to come into being, sprawling with a thousand limbs all over this world. The giant—so small to us now—is stirring, is turning. The moment is critical. Its cantankerous, cancerous cells, run wild, are threatening to exhaust and poison the whole organism. But, as always in evolution, co-operation, in the long run, must win out over conflict; diversity in unity, over chaos. They are trying for a new inner equilibrium, a new organization, a new specialization. Maleness and femaleness, obviously, are undergoing displacements, restratifications, in the process.

Conflict, at this point, is plainly anti-evolutionary. There can be no question about that. Co-operation is the password to the further progress of the human-superhuman species. But whenever evolution proceeds through co-operation, we have seen, it proceeds through the female. Group-maker from the beginning, the female thrives on the forces which the group, in turn, releases: evolution's archaic-futuristic child.

We are still rising. The earthball is getting smaller and smaller. Now we are ready to take off for the boundless realm of the future.

My Own Utopia

*So then, as God can create what He will, so can He
change the nature of what He has created at His
good pleasure. And . . . the alteration of the known
nature of any creature into a nature unknown, is
not opposite unto the laws of nature.*

ST. AUGUSTINE[1]

*For the Lord Himself, being asked by a certain per-
son when His kingdom would come, said, When
the two shall be one, and the outside as the inside,
and the male with the female, neither male nor
female.*

ST. CLEMENS ROMANUS[2]

We have seen that on every level of experience, conscious and subconscious, there is an association, an affinity, between the female and the collective. This is just a phase, an aspect, of the more complex phenomenon—the interpenetrability, the reciprocal transformability that exists between the individual and the group—a phenomenon the primitive felt, and we know.

To me, this gives an immense feeling of relief, of peace with the universe, of confidence. For me, this awareness closes a wound that was opened when I was quite small.

I still remember it as if it had happened yesterday; forty years have passed in the meantime.

My little brother was two years old, and I was three. We were dressed alike, in our party frocks: a sort of Russian blouse, belted, over shorts. We had the same hairdo: bangs, in page fashion. Our parents were entertaining some guests at tea, and at a certain moment we were called in to greet the guests like good little children and to eat some cookies in return for good behavior.

My mother was proud of us. How cute, the guests said. Are they twins? No, one year apart. . . . Two little boys? No, a boy and a girl. I still hear the voices ringing in my ear.

At that moment my mother felt like teasing the guests. She often did. Which one is the boy and which one is the girl? she challenged them. I bet you, you'll never guess. But the guests did not hesitate. "This one is the boy," the lady said, pointing at my brother. *"He looks more serious."*

That shocked me. It dug a little wound into my little brain, and the wound grew as the brain grew. Why should boys *look* more serious than girls? Why should boys *be* more serious than girls? Why should boys *be taken* more seriously than girls?

Whenever my little brother and I were presented to guests after that—tea guests, lunch guests, dinner guests—I put on the most formidable frown a child is capable of. I was dead serious. For the photographers, too. I still have series of baby pictures and family pictures at home, with that formidable frown on my face.

Among my parents' guests for whom I put it on, years later, there was a great French pacifist, a woman, who somehow impressed me. I guess that is why I tried to frown especially impressively for her. "What do you call her?" the guest asked my parents. *Medi;* which, in Bavarian, means "little girl." "Medi?" the guest repeated. "You should call her 'Meditation'! *She looks so serious!"*

Encouraged by this success, I looked positively grim from then on. A picture, taken during a vacation in France when I was eighteen, shows me exhibiting the mood of one just escaped from the worst penitentiary and set on ultimate rapine and murder.

I felt grim, too. I wanted to be a musician. I was full of music, and I worked hard. But looking around, and looking behind, what did I see?

Women cannot be great musicians.

I fell in love, a romantic, unreachable love, and was sent to a psychiatrist. "You are an artist," he kindly said, to distract me from my sorrows. "Make up your mind. Choose between your art and your man, between yourself and just ordinary wifehood."

Fiddlesticks. Did anyone ever tell Toscanini, or Bach, that he had to choose between music and family, between art and a normal life? Besides, what was the use of renouncing the one, if you are condemned by nature to mediocrity in the other?

I never believed in renouncing anyway. I believe in rebellion. To bow to universal injustice seemed to make no more sense than to believe in universal justice.

It took me about twenty years: a marriage, and its end; the raising of daughters, who now are young women. But I am at peace now, with myself, with women in general, and with this world, of which we are a phase, a passing phase. Our relationships to this world are like a mathematical function that has its graph, its curve—that is beyond justice and injustice. What a sense of peace, of reconciliation, this gives.

Look at this graph, this stretch of curve, this abstract design. Measure its co-ordinates here, measure them there, construct its equation, its function; you can continue the graph, prolong it, to infinity. What a sense of power.

Here is the piece of graph behind us:

The beginning of life was sexless. When sexual reproduction came into existence, multiplying the possibilities of hereditary combinations and speeding up evolution, male and female alike expelled their sexual products into the surrounding waters. Fertilization was external; external the maturation of the fertilized egg. Left to chance and circumstance were birth and the development of the young.

Then fertilization was internalized. Copulation came into existence. But the maturation of the fertilized egg was still external; external, birth and growth of the young.

Then gestation was internalized, and the mammal came into being.

First the embryo was expelled at an early stage and carried externally, as in a marsupial pouch; then internal gestation was prolonged over ever greater periods of development: the young animal, calf or horse, was born to the light in almost perfect shape, and ready to cope with life on its own terms after but a few months.

Now we are at the turning point. Now we see the curve bend. *Homo sapiens* is the last mammal. There won't be other mammals after him. His baby, far from perfect, is helpless, unfinished, like the little marsupial. But the mother, to whom he is so long attached, is at the end of her mammality. Especially in the higher classes, in the cities, among intellectual and professional women—among the most evolved specimens, the leaders of the species—breast-milk is scarce. It is not a question of lack of good will: they want to nurse their babies. How they enjoy this unique experience. But when they come home from the hospital, get up and go about their usual chores, the milk disappears and there's nothing they can do.

Now, science is mighty and will be mightier yet; so there is no reason why it could not stimulate, reactivate those atrophied mammalian glands.

However, nursing, while being wonderful, is also very confining. It interferes with work schedules and social engagements—a cumbersome joy in the long run. And since there are now the formulas and the bottles, and since doctors—though periodically contradicted by the voice of reaction—assure us that a scientifically prepared bottle formula is better, safer, than the natural, often imperfect product of tired, nervous, harassed mothers . . .

So lactation is being externalized.

And since lactation can be externalized without any hazard, the maturation of the infant is being externalized—in nursery schools, day nurseries, and crèches—a month after the child is born. Society, group-planning, is taking the place of chance and natural surroundings. So mother can go to work. It is inevitable.

Of course, the more work there is for mother, the more hazardous becomes gestation. Premature births are common.

Mother's physical build—tall and slender—does not seem particularly suitable for childbearing and childbirth labor.

But premature births are no longer so dangerous as they used to be. There are incubators.

Gestation is being externalized—the incubator plus formula, corresponding to the egg.

Then, in 1961, thirty years after Aldous Huxley wrote *Brave New World,* Professor Daniele Angelo Petrucci in Bologna reported that he had successfully fertilized a human ovum in a test tube and raised the embryo for twenty-nine days. The Church frowned. The professor discontinued the experiment. The fetus is gone, but the feat remains.

Fertilization has been externalized, with the test tube taking the place of the primeval waters, and scientific planning superseding chance.

There is nothing frightening in all this. Why must we view the future as a nightmare—an air-conditioned nightmare, if you wish? *Homo sapiens* has come, *Homo sapiens* will go. He could go either of two ways. He could go the way the sabertooth and mammoth went, or some other prehistoric animals, who developed such formidable weapons that, equipped only to kill but not to live, they simply died out—bypassed by evolution. The superindividual that is human society is not growing such an armature. Maybe it will go the way of the sabertooth and mammoth. But the sabertooth was utterly helpless in the face of his destiny; man is not. Evolution is in our hands. "Through billions of years of blind mutation, pressing against the shifting walls of their environment," Professor Herman J. Muller, Nobel prize–winning geneticist of the University of Indiana says, "microbes finally emerged as man. We are no longer blind; at least we are beginning to be conscious of what has happened and of what may happen. From now on evolution is what we make it. . . ."[3]

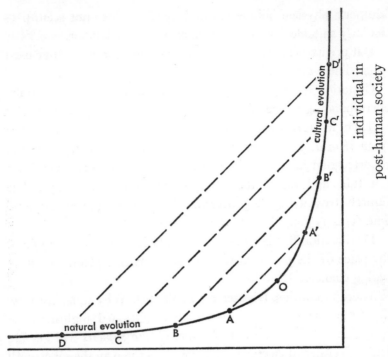

origin of individual
in animal kingdom

O = internal fertilization
internal gestation,
maternal lactation

A=egg	A′=incubator
B=external fertilization in nature	B′=external scientific fertilization
C=sex reversal : male-female	C′=sex reversal : female-male
D=pre-sexual organisms	D′=post-sexual organisms

Curve shows transition from natural evolution to cultural evolution and its acceleration. It also shows how each point in cultural evolution has its corresponding point (the distance from the vertex being the same) in natural evolution: the farther up we move on the curve of cultural evolution, the farther *back* we have to look for the corresponding point in natural evolution. This is valid for biological evolution as it is true, even more obviously, for psychological evolution.

Of course it will be a World State, a federal republic; for the earth has become too small, physically and spiritually, to stand divided.

This is not the place to discuss the constitutional mechanism of such a world republic. Suffice it to indicate that it will be strongly centralized in basic questions concerning all its members, and loosely decentralized in all other matters.

The earth will be inhabited by only one race; for all races will merge—the best features of each to be maintained in the emerging new race, whose people will be tall, strong, dark-skinned, dark-eyed, with large, vaulted skulls and small jaws.

There will be no ceiling on wealth—why should there?—but there will be a floor, a high floor, under poverty. The poor shall no longer be with us; for food, housing, energy, heat, clothing, medical care, insurance, social security, education, transportation, will be free for everyone. The progress of science and technology, the tapping of the unlimited resources of the universe, combined with a rational organization of labor and a controlled system of planning and distribution, will make this possible. And what with the progress of automation, all this common wealth will be produced with very little human labor: two to three hours a day in a five-day week; plus the labor draft of four years.

The leisure class, as we know, will be the leisure mass. Why should that frighten us? That men do not know what to do with their spare time strikes me as a puny and short-lived problem. It has taken hundreds of thousands of years to make of man the hard-working, competitive animal that he is. It will take

much less time for him to lose this acquired character and accept leisure as a natural state. Behold the fowls of the air: for
they sow not, neither do they reap. Consider the lilies of the
field: they toil not, neither do they spin.

In his spare time, now dreaded and coveted like sin, every
man will be an artist, every man will be a philosopher. The re-
lease from drudgery and slavery will make men really human,
bent on the true, the good, and the beautiful.

Children will be born, I hesitate to say, pretty much along the
lines suggested satirically by Huxley in *Brave New World,* and
more seriously by the above-quoted Herman Muller, by Haldane[4] and others. There will be great establishments, where
banks of deep-frozen reproductive cells, both male and female,
will be maintained, along with multiplying cultures of them.
This procedure will make the most precious genetic heritage of
all humanity available for nurturing into childhood and
adulthood.

Let us most fervently hope that the transition to this type of
procreation will not be hastened by the genetic unfitness of a
large part of the population due to an atomic holocaust. The
deformation of pregnancy and the hazards of viviparous birth,
at any rate, will be remembered as simply beastly.

But I do not think we will breed alphas, epsilons, and semi-
moronic gamma-minuses, as Huxley fancies. We do not need
immutable castes, ant-like, in our society to come; that society,
far from stunting individual development, will create a new,
specifically human, synthesis of individualism and collectivism.

We will breed only the best: all alpha-pluses.

At the age of two, or thereabouts, these children will leave
the Establishment and be adopted by family groups. For the
raising of children will be a favorite hobby of the leisure mass
—the beauty of children, the contact with the magic world of
children, a main source of their inspiration.

There will be no difference between boys and girls. They will be children, that is all. They will all have the same education, the same way of dressing, the same games, the same purpose in life. Imagine them romping, on a holiday, in the playground, where centrifugal accelerators and pressure-shoots, modeled on those that prepared the cosmonauts and astronauts for their adventures, will have taken the place of the old merry-go-rounds and Ferris wheels. For all the children will be getting ready to be spacemen, one day.

Between the ages of eighteen and twenty, when their primary education is completed, they will *all* grow to be *women*. For to be a woman no longer means to bear children. Femininity will rise out of social context and reflect a psychological, a psychosomatic condition.[5] These women will be tall and strong and beautiful, like Michelangelo's angels. They will bear the brunt of the work in this new world. During the four years of the labor draft they will learn how the economy of this world state ticks, from the lowest echelons to the highest. Drafted women will be burdened with whatever drudgery is left in agriculture and industry and services.

When they come back from the labor draft, the women will be scientists, doctors, professional women, business executives, administrators, educators, and social workers. The bulk of the international income will go through their hands; which means, they will be an enormous political power. Their power, and their experience, will carry them into public office: practically all positions of the executive branch of government will be filled by women, including that of President of the World Republic. The collectivist character of this new society brings that with it; there's no way of getting around it. But let no one fear: these women will be fully suited to their high position—by birth, by character, and upbringing.

When they get out of the labor draft, the women will also be ready to found families. (Where the men come from we shall see shortly.) These families, obviously, will have little in common with the closed, patriarchal family of our own time. The post-individual family, like the pre-individual family, will be a group; an open group, including six to fifteen adults and four to six children each.

The family will be a working community, dedicated to all those types of work that are not owned or run by the State: all work that embellishes the life of the community, from fancy cooking to all the arts and crafts, fashion, dance, drama, music, plastic arts, poetry, philosophy. Much of the family work will be done for and with the children: the creation of myth and lore, of new forms of art, of new forms of play and happiness.

Although the products of this work may and will enter into commerce, enriching the family and raising its standard of living, the family is not founded primarily on economic interests but on a community of taste and on the common pursuit of the true and the beautiful. This, the women—who are young, fair, receptive, willing to sacrifice, loyal, eager to serve—will learn from the men, who are older, more mature: "capable of communicating wisdom and virtue," while the young women are "seeking to acquire them with a view to education and wisdom." And when physical love and spiritual love thus coincide, "and meet in one, then, and only then, may the beloved," in our case, the woman, "yield with honor to the lover," in our case, the man.

The words between quotation marks are taken—the reader may guess—from Plato's *Symposium*. And the love between men and women, in our post-individual community, will indeed be Platonic, in that it will unite physical and spiritual love and will be aimed at creating beauty immortal, rather than mortal children. Love will be harmony, the reconciliation of elements that are not opposite, but harmonized. For men and women, in our society, cannot be considered as opposite elements.

The men, as we said, will be older—between forty-five and seventy-five years old—and more experienced than the women.

They will be the masters, the teachers, the inspirers of women. They will be the great inventors and explorers. They will be the great artists and architects. In public life they will fill all the positions in the legislative branch of government as well as in the lower judiciary. But Supreme Court justices, the great historians and prophets, the high priests of the new society, will be human beings past seventy-five, up to, say, one hundred years of age, who will be neither male nor female—individuals rich in three or four life experiences, and approaching a perfection and greatness unknown at present.

When the children in a family have all grown into young women, gone away from home, joined the labor force; when the men have either died—which, owing to the advanced state of medicine, will occur only quite exceptionally—or, what may happen more commonly, are missing in the cosmos; or when the men have become sexless superindividuals: then, of course, comes the moment for a woman to grow and mature into manhood. The transition will be smooth and spontaneous. The woman, who is now about forty-five years old, has had a full life, has raised her children, has learned from the man she loves, whose disciple she was, what she was able to learn. If now she is herself "capable of communicating wisdom and virtue," she will naturally feel attracted toward a young person "seeking to acquire them." She will grow into the position of a man; she will become a man.*

* Nietzsche anticipated something of this type of changing relationship when, in *Human, All too Human,* he suggests that every man marry twice: an older, experienced woman, when he is in his twenties, and a young girl, when he is in his thirties, after which marriage is a dangerous nuisance anyway. "Thus one might wonder whether Nature and Reason would not suggest to man several successive marriages, in such a way that at first, at the age of twenty-one or thereabout, he should marry an older woman, his superior intellectually and morally, who would become his guide through the dangers besetting his 'twenties (ambition, hate, self-contempt, passions of all sorts). The love of this woman would transform itself later into a purely motherly love; and not only would she tolerate, she would most wholesomely want her man, now in his thirties, to enter into relationship with a younger woman whose education he could take into his hands. Marriage is an institution that

We have seen, in Chapter I, how sex reversal is common on the lowest levels of life, and how, in forms in which sex reversal is usual, the physiological state established by the hereditary constitution is readily overridden through the environment: how, before becoming *caste,* sex was *phase.* Remember our remote ancestor, the "boatshell" snails of the genus *Crepidula:* after a juvenile period that is essentially asexual, Professor Allee tells us, the growing *Crepidula* first becomes a male, and later, sometimes only at long last, transforms into a female—femaleness, at that stage of evolution, being the crown of success of life.

Here we would have one more instance where a point on the upper part of our graph exactly corresponds to a point on the lower part: sex reversal, from male to female, on the lower curve, where crowding masculinizes; and sex reversal, from female to male, on the upper curve, where crowding feminizes. Somewhere in the middle, we find, according to Professor Wheeler, a good many kinds of fish—our close relatives—who are usually female in their youth, and, when older, turn into males.

We have seen beasts changing sex, under the biochemical action of "social hormones." We have seen gods changing sex, under the subconscious action of social context. Why should we be amazed at seeing human beings do the same? Magic, plus social context, has wrought sex reversal on prophets and shamans. Biochemistry, plus social context, may achieve as much.*

---

is necessary between twenty and thirty, useful between thirty and forty; but in later years it often becomes harmful and causes a process of spiritual involution in man."

* "From the words 'Till we all come to a perfect man, to the measure of the age and the fullness of Christ,' and from the words 'conformed to the image of the Son of God,' some conclude that women shall not resurrect as women, but that all shall be men, because God made man only of earth and woman of the man."—St. Augustine, *City of God.*

But evolution, on our graph, ever open, runs no risk of turning into involution, and none of the gains made in the process are sacrificed.*

Not all women, of course, will arrive at the turning point, at least at the beginning. Only the better, the more gifted ones will get there—which, in a collectivist society, will be the majority. A minority, however, will not make the grade; at least for some time to come. They will remain women, will age as women. Individual failure, seen from an individual angle. The action of the group-*Gestalt* on the sex balance, seen from the statistical point of view—the physiology of numbers.

The group-force in a collectivist society, as we have seen, engenders a numerical superiority of females. Thus, women will comprise the entire age group from eighteen to forty-five, plus, let us say, thirty per cent of the age group, forty-five–seventy-five; that is, sixty-five per cent of the sexually mature population. Men will compromise seventy per cent of the age group, forty-five–seventy-five; that is, thirty-five per cent of the sexually mature population. This proportion should fairly reflect the degree of basic collectivism and marginal individualism of society, during the initial phase.

It may be easily imagined that the women above forty-five will not command the highest respect of the community. They will be considered as failures in life, as "arrested men," to use a term coined by Herbert Spencer for women in general. We may even fancy that in moments of tension, of mass hysteria,

---

* It occurs to me that this evolutionary curve, tracing *forth* what has been traced *back* since the origin of life, with the never-ending and the never-beginning meeting at an imaginary point, expresses something very analogous to what Hermann Broch expressed poetically in the archemythical dream of death agony in *The Death of Vergil*. The soul of the dying poet, *rising* through various stages of its ontogenetic liberation to eternity, is at the same time *descending*, backward, through the phylogenetic stages of evolution: from being human, it becomes mammal, bird, fish, mollusk, primordial-ultimate nonbeing.

which can develop whenever the collectivist component of our social psychology overpowers the individualist—that in such moments these poor aging women may be persecuted as witches. ... As this society moves toward a perfect equilibrium between individualism and collectivism, between male and female components, this group of unfortunate women will disappear, and all women will mature to manhood. The proportion between men and women will then be one to one.

Strange new world. And yet, not so strange, after all. If only we get used to the idea that mankind is bound to change, is not the end of evolution, which has no end; if we think, on the other hand, that what is new and yet to come, is present, pre-designed in the old.

What we have foreseen—that is, seen—in these last few pages, is the rise of a global superorganism of which every human being is a cell.

In the superorganism of the ant hill, each "cell" has its fixed place and function: some are reproductive organs, others ingest the food for the community, others form the tentacles, or the aggressive and defensive weapons of the organism. Each caste is fixed and frozen. The individual is nothing. Change is abolished. The female is supreme.

In our human superorganism, co-operation will be as total as in the ant state. Conflict will be eliminated. But what was static in the ant state will become dynamic. The "caste system," instead of limiting and specializing individual development, will round it out and enrich it. Each cell is the whole organism. Each individual is the whole society, every aspect of it. The caste system has become a "phase system." So total indeed is social mobility, which is change-promoting, that it includes sexual mobility: its logical extension.

As the contrast between group and individual will disappear

—the total group fostering the total individual—so will the contrast between female and male; and every individual will be both: female, then male, then their synthesis. In such a society, to quote Julian Huxley again, "the idea of stability [coinciding, in our scheme with *group, female*] and change [*individual, male*] tend to become combined in the ideal of integrated process: the moving equilibrium of an ordered transformation."[6]

Prophecies and dreams have no time dimension. What shall exist already exists. Once-upon-a-time is no time and always.

When I read:

Modern civilization is becoming industrial, that is to say, feminine in character, for the industries belonged primitively to women, and they tend to make men like women.[7]

When I read:

Many women now think as the crowd thinks, and they believe in crowd opinion. . . . Society has taken on many things that women used to do, the care of the young and the sick and the old, the necessary care of the individual. So strange are the shifts of modern times that not only are women less feminine . . . but it is now society that has become feminine. Social legislation has taken on much of woman's former role, social feeling includes and comforts all, the crowd manners are warm and welcoming. . . .[8]

When I read:

Three fourths of the American economic power [the greatest in the world!] in in the hands of women. Women hold sixty-five per cent of the shares of all the great companies, seventy per cent of the insurance policies, sixty-five per cent of savings accounts. . . . American politics are dominated by women. In 1958 the Census Bureau stated that women voters exceeded men voters by four million and a half. A presidential candidate must please the women above all. Almost the entire cultural life is dominated by women: the teaching profession (sixty-five per cent of all teachers are women); the galleries (eighty-four per cent are run by women);

the theaters (sixty-three per cent), movies and TV (fifty-eight per cent). . . . The American woman is really a man. . . . In 1940 there were a million and a half more women than men. According to current estimates, there will be seven million and a half more women than men in 1975. . . .[9]

When I read:

Very roughly summarizing the findings of one census: there is a very marked influence of occupation on the masculine-feminine score. . . . Culture tends to make man's mind resemble woman's; intelligence and education to make woman's mind resemble man's. . . .[10]

When I read:

The problem of women represents only one particular instance exemplifying the transition from the individualism of a liberal society to the organization of a planned society. Before the development of individualism, the problem of women's emancipation and, concurrently, the enquiry into her aptitudes, could not arise; after its decline and the move towards a society which thinks primarily in terms of social welfare, it could, in its original form, not survive. Only a liberalistic ideology, with the emphasis on individual achievements, created an atmosphere in which the question was primarily focused on psychological abilities. . . .[11]

When I read:

There are no women of genius. Women of genius are all men. . . .[12]

—then I know we are on a right track. I won't say, *the* right track, because there are infinitely many tracks, the future being infinite-dimensional. But a right track it must be, for I could mark a point on my graph for each one of these statements. And those who made them—Havelock Ellis, Florida Scott-Maxwell, Oriana Fallaci, Terman and Miles, Viola Klein, Edmond and Jules Goncourt, in this order—did not write in and of their time, our time, only, but they wrote of my Utopia, in my Utopia.

The family is in crisis. Children are delinquent. Wives are alienated, frustrated. Whether divorce should be facilitated or rendered more difficult; whether woman should work or keep house; what kind of work she should do; whether babies should be born at the hospital or at home, in pain or under anaesthesia: these are questions that seem eternal and are fleeting, like dreams. Theory upon theory is offered. Society stirs in a nightmare, turns from the left to the right, from stomach to back, but finds no peace. It dreams of the integrating force of religions that are dead, of the unique value given to the life of woman by her unique, mystic and dolorous experience of childbirth.

But if science, potentially, has abolished pain, then pain has become something immoral. If science, potentially, has abolished childbirth, it is useless to seek mystical gratification in it, a justification of feminine being. We are on the move toward a new species which, even before coming into being, is on the move toward a new new species.

I have tried to imagine it. Let us try to imagine it—but not under the wicked assumption that it will lose all the good features of our human species while perpetuating all its bad ones! Why? In the long run, co-operation has always prevailed over conflict, which is lack of co-operation. In the long run, even disruptive, destructive inventions have always turned out socially good and useful. *"Pessimism is the result of incomplete knowledge or of too short a view. Any general or long-run pessimism is contradicted by the facts of evolution and progress in the past."*

NOTES

PROLOGUE: CREDO-VEDO

1. Julian Huxley, "Cultural Process and Evolution," in *Behavior and Evolution,* ed. Anne Roe and George Gaylord Simpson (New Haven, 1958).

ONE: THE BIRDS AND THE BEES

1. Warder C. Allee, *Cooperation Among Animals* (New York, 1951).
2. *Ibid.*
3. *Ibid.*
4. *Ibid.*
5. Alfred Emerson in *Behavior and Evolution,* ed. Anne Roe and George Gaylord Simpson (New Haven, 1958).
6. Charles Elton, *Mice, Voles and Lemmings* (Oxford, 1942).
7. Walter Heape, *Emigration, Migration and Nomadism* (Cambridge, 1931).
8. Julian Huxley, H. G. Wells and G. P. Wells, *The Science of Life* (London, 1929).
9. Warder C. Allee, *op. cit.*
10. Jacobus Christian Faure, *The Phases of Locusts in South Africa* (London, 1932).
11. Sigmund Freud, *Group Psychology and the Analysis of the Ego* (London, 1922).
12. Maurice Maeterlinck, *The Life of the Bee* (New York, 1901); *The Life of the Ant* (New York, 1930).
13. Karl von Frisch, *Bees: Their Vision, Chemical Senses, and Language* (Ithaca, 1950); *The Dancing Bees: An Account of the Life and Senses of the Honey Bee* (London, 1954).
14. Theodore C. Schneirla, *Learning and Orientation in Ants* (Baltimore, 1929).
15. William M. Wheeler, *Social Life among the Insects* (New York, 1923).
16. *Ibid.*
17. Warder C. Allee, *op. cit.*
18. For all aspects of woman's physical superiority see: Ashley Montagu, *The Natural Superiority of Women* (New York, 1953).

See also:
Warder C. Allee, *Concerning the Origin of Sociality in Animals* (Chicago, 1940); *Animal Sociology* (Encyclopaedia Brittanica); *Animal Aggregations* (Chicago, 1931).
F. Alverdes, *Social Life in the Animal World* (New York, 1927).
F. J. J. Buytendijk, *Mensch and Tier* (Hamburg, 1958).
Frank F. Darling, *A Herd of Red Deer* (London, 1937).
Julian Huxley, *Evolution, the Modern Synthesis* (London, 1942).
W. P. Pycraft, *The Courtship of Animals* (London, 1914).
Adolf Renane, *Das soziale Leben der Tiere* (Hamburg, 1961).
A. H. Sturtevant and T. Dobzhansky, *Geographical Distribution and Cytology of Sex Ratio* (Washington, 1931).

TWO: WOMEN AND CROWDS

1. Florida Scott-Maxwell, *Women, and Sometimes Men* (New York, 1957).
2. Kurt Lewin, *Field Theory in Social Science* (New York, 1951).
3. Alfred Sauvy, "On the Relation Between Domination and the Number of Men," *Diogenes* (Paris, 1953).
4. John Elof Boodin, *The Social Mind. Foundations of Social Philosophy* (New York, 1939).
5. David Riesman, *The Lonely Crowd* (New Haven, 1950).
6. Sigmund Freud, *Group Psychology and the Analysis of the Ego* (London, 1922).
7. Philippe de Félice, *Foules en Délire. Extrases collectives. Essai sur quelques formes inferieurs de la mystique* (Paris, 1947).
8. Gustave Le Bon, *La Psychologie des Foules* (Paris, 1895).
9. José Ortega y Gasset, *The Revolt of the Masses* (New York, 1932).
10. Paul Reiwald, *Vom Geist der Massen* (Zurich, 1946).
11. Gustave Le Bon, *op. cit.*
12. Denis Diderot, *On Women* (London, 1927).
13. Johann Wolfgang von Goethe, *Faust, Part 2*. G. M. Priest, tr. (Chicago, 1952).
14. Adolph Hitler, *Mein Kampf* (Munich, 1927).
15. Friedrich Nietzsche, *Human, All Too Human* (New York, 1927).
16. Havelock Ellis, *Man and Woman, A Study of Human Secondary Sexual Character* (London, 1930).
17. Gina Lombroso and Guglielmo Ferrero, *La donna delinquente, la prostituta, e la donna normale* (Milan, 1915).
18. William Butler Yeats, *Dramatis Personae* (Dublin, 1935).
19. Cicero, *De Republica*.
20. Martin Luther, *A Vindication of Married Life*.
21. Havelock Ellis, *op. cit.*

22. Cicero, *De Oratore.*

23. Aristophanes, *The Thesmophoriazusae.*

24. Sigmund Freud, *Three Essays on Sexuality* (London, 1953).

25. Helene Deutsch, *Psychology of Women* (New York, 1944).

26. *Ibid.*

27. Sigmund Freud, *op. cit.*

28. Otto Weininger, *Geschlecht und Charakter* (Leipzig, 1920).

29. Alfred Adler, *Social Interest: A Challenge to Mankind* (London, 1938).

30. Paul Reiwald, *op. cit.*

31. Thomas E. Bowdich, *Essay on Superstitions, Customs, and Ways Common to the Ancient Egyptians, Abyssinians and Ashantees* (Paris, 1821).

32. Thomas Hobbes, *The Leviathan.*

33. Viola Klein, *The Feminine Character* (London, 1946).

34. Clara Thompson, "Cultural Pressures on the Psychology of Women" (*Psychology*, V, 1942).

35. Viola Klein, *op. cit.*

36. F. A. Moss, *Comparative Psychology* (New York, 1946).

37. Ashley Montague, *The Natural Superiority of Women* (New York, 1953).

38. Aldous Huxley, *Brave New World Revisited* (New York, 1958).

39. Erich Kahler, *Man the Measure* (New York, 1943).

40. Florida Scott-Maxwell, *op. cit.*

41. Havelock Ellis, *op. cit.*

42. Johann Jakob Bachofen, *Das Mutterrecht. Eine Untersuchung ueber die Gynokratie der alten Welt nach ihrer religioesen und rechtlichen Natur.* (Basel, 1861).

43. *Ibid.*

44. *Ibid.*

See also:

Anna Brownell Jameson, *Characteristics of Women* (London, 1835).

Margaret Mead, *Male and Female* (New York, 1949).

Paul J. A. Moebius, *Ueber den physiologischen Schwachsinn des Weibes* (Halle, 1907).

William I. Thomas, *Sex and Society: Studies in the Social Psychology of Sex* (Chicago, 1907).

THREE: IN HEAVEN AS ON EARTH

1. Erich Neumann, *The Great Mother* (New York, 1955).

2. G. A. Barton, *The Religions of the World* (Chicago, 1942).

3. J. J. Bachofen, *Das Mutterrecht* (Basel, 1861).

4. Robert Briffault, *The Mothers. The Matriarchal Theory of Social Origin* (New York, 1931).

5. Friedrich Engels, *The Origin of the Family, Private Property, and the State* (Chicago, 1902).

6. Erich Neumann, *op. cit.*

7. Phyllis Kaberry, *Aboriginal Women, Sacred and Profane*. (London, 1949).

8. Hermann Baumann, *Das Doppelte Geschlecht. Ethnologische Studien zur Bisexualitaet in Ritus und Mythos* (Berlin, 1955).

9. Euripedes, *Alcestis*.

10. J. J. Bachofen, *op. cit.*

11. G. A. Barton, *op. cit.*

12. Morris Jastrow, *The Religion of Babylonia and Assyria* (Boston, 1898).

13. James H. Breasted, *A History of Egypt from the Earliest Times to the Persian Conquest*. (New York, 1905).

14. J. J. Bachofen, *op. cit.*

15. Otto Weininger, *Geschlecht und Charakter* (Leipzig, 1920).

16. Martin Luther, *A Vindication of Married Life*.

17. Emile Durkheim, *Les formes élémentaires de la vie religieuse* (Paris, 1912).

18. William Robertson Smith, *Kinship and Marriage in Early Arabia* (London, 1883).

19. Bronislaw Malinowski, *Magic, Science and Religion* (Boston, 1948).

20. Euripides, *Bacchanals*.

21. *Ibid.*

22. *Ibid.*

23. *Ibid.*

24. J. J. Bachofen, *op. cit.*

25. E. Neumann, *op. cit.*

See also:

Mary Esther Harding, *The Way of all Women* (New York, 1933); *Women's Mysteries, Ancient and Modern* (New York, 1955).

Otis Mason, *Women's Share in Primitive Culture* (New York, 1897).

Thomas F. Thiselton-Dyer, *Folklore of Women* (London, 1905).

FOUR: LA LINGUA BATTE DOVE IL DENTE DUOLE

1. Bronislaw Malinowski, *Magic, Science and Religion* (Boston, 1948).

2. K. Bruggmann, *Grundriss der vergleichenden Grammatik der Indogermanischen Sprachen* (Strassburg, 1897).

3. Johannes Schmidt, *Die Pluralbildung der Indogermanischen Neutra* (Weimar, 1890).

4. Morris Jastrow, *The Religion of Babylonia and Assyria* (Boston, 1898).

5. Aldous Huxley, *Brave New World* (New York, 1932).

6. Simone de Beauvoir, *The Second Sex* (London, 1953).

7. Carlo Tagliavini, *Modificazioni del Linguaggio nella Parlata delle donne* (Padua, 1943).

8. Otto Jesperson, *Language, Its Nature, Development and Origin* (New York, 1921).

9. Edward Sapir, *Male and Female Forms of Speech in Yana. Notes on the Culture of the Yanas* (Berkeley, 1943).

10. Carlo Tagliavini, *op. cit.*

FIVE: WOMEN AND THE FACE OF THE CROWD

1. Gertrude Stein, *Picasso* (Boston, 1959).

2. Peter Strieder, *Das Volk auf Deutschen Tafelbildern des ausgehenden Mittelalters* (Munich, 1939).

3. Roger Fry, *Vision and Design* (London, 1920).

4. Deoclesio Redig Da Campo, *Il Giudizio Universale de Michelangelo* (Vatican, 1944).

5. Paul Haessaerts, *James Ensor* (Milan, 1961).

6. Werner Haftman, *Malerei im 20, Jahrhundert* (Munich, 1955).

7. Sophie Drinker, *Music and Women* (New York, 1948).

8. Erich Neumann, *The Great Mother* (New York, 1955).

SIX: WOMEN IN NEVERLAND

1. Oscar Wilde, "The Soul of Man under Socialism," *The Complete Writings of Oscar Wilde* (New York, 1909).

2. William I. Thomas, *Sex and Society: Studies in the Social Psychology of Sex* (Chicago, 1907).

3. Julian Huxley, *Evolution, the Modern Synthesis* (London, 1942).

4. Plato, *The Republic.*

5. Aldous Huxley, *Brave New World* (New York, 1932).

6. Cicero, *De Republica.*

7. Thomas More, *Utopia.*

8. Francis Bacon, *New Atlantis.*

9. Tommaso Campanella, *The City of the Sun.*

10. Muriel Hughes, *Women Healers in Medieval Life and Literature* (New York, 1943).

11. Tommaso Campanella, *Political Aphorisms* (Turin, 1961).

SEVEN: THE FEMININE REVOLUTION

1. Auguste Comte, *Catéchisme positiviste* (Paris, 1852).

2. Hans Hinterhäuser, *Utopie und Wirklichkeit bei Diderot* (Heidelberg, 1957).

3. Marie Jean de Condorcet, *Esquisse d'un tableau historique des progrès de l'esprit humain* (Paris, 1793).

4. John Stuart Mill, *The Subjection of Women* (London, 1869).

5. Charles Fourier, *Théorie de l'unité universelle,* Second Edition (Paris, 1841-43).

6. *Ibid.*

7. *Ibid.*

8. *Ibid.*

9. Robert Owen, *A New View of Society and Other Writings* (London, 1927).

10. Claude Henri de Saint-Simon, *Lettres d'un habitant de Geneve, Du système industriel,* in *Oeuvres de Saint-Simon e d'Enfantin* (Paris, 1863-78).

11. Enfantin–Saint-Simon, *Science de l'homme* (Paris, 1858).

12. *Ibid.*

13. Gabriel de Fogni, *Les aventures de Jacques Sadaut dans la ecouverte e le voiage de la Terre Australe* (Paris, 1692).

14. E. Schomann, *Franzoesische Utopisten des 18. Jahrhunderts und ihr Frauenideal* (Berlin, 1911).

15. W. H. Hudson, *A Crystal Age* (New York, 1906).

16. Lewis Mumford, *The Story of Utopia* (New York, 1941).

17. Jean Jacques Rousseau, *The Social Contract.*

18. Jean Jacques Rousseau, *Discourse on Political Economy.*

19. François de Salignac de la Mothe Fénelon, *Instructions for the Education of Daughters* (Glasgow, 1750).

20. Denis Diderot, *Supplement au voyage de Bougainville, ou Dialogue entre A et B sur l'inconvenience d'attacher des idées morales a certaines actions physiques, qui n'en comportent par, 1771.* (Paris, 1921).

21. Denis Diderot, *Fragment échappés, oeuvres complètes* (Paris, 1875). For all the foregoing, see Hans Hinterhäuser, *op. cit.*

22. Friedrich Nietzsche, *Beyond Good and Evil; Human, All Too Human. Complete Works* (New York, 1910–27).

23. Erich Kahler, *Culture and Evolution* (New York, 1960).

24. August Bebel, *Die Frau und der Sozialismus* (Stuttgart, 1895).

25. Anton V. Nemilov, *The Biological Tragedy of Woman* (New York, 1932).

26. N. Lenin, *Selected Works,* Vol. IX (New York, 1939).

27. Piotr Alekseyevich Kropotkin, *Mutual Aid, A Factor of Evolution* (London, 1902).

28. Warder C. Allee, *Animal Sociology* (Chicago, 1948).

29. *Ibid.*

30. Warder C. Allee, *Cooperation Among Animals* (New York, 1951).

See also:

C. C. A. Bouglé, *Chez les prophètes socialistes* (Paris, 1918).

Karl Mannheim, *Ideology and Utopia* (New York, 1936).

Jules Michelet, *Die Frauen der Revolution* (Munich, 1913).

G. B. Shaw, *The Intelligent Woman's Guide to Socialism and Capitalism* (London, 1928).

EIGHT: ASCENT OF WOMAN: LOWER REACHES

1. Simone de Beauvoir, *The Second Sex* (New York, 1953).
2. Corrado Tumiati, *Nessuno Risponde* (Florence, 1950).
3. *Rinascita: La Donna in Italia* (Rome, 1961).
4. Anna Garofalo, *L'Italiana in Italia* (Bari, 1956).
5. Cesare Alessandri, *Il lavoro femminile nel regime fascista* (Rocca di S. Casciano, 1938).
6. Clifford Kirkpatrick, *Nazi Germany: Its Women and Family Life* (Indianapolis-New York, 1938).
7. J. T. Headley, *Letters from Italy* (New York, 1848).
8. Arthur Calhoun, *A Social History of the American Family from Colonial Times to the Present* (Cleveland, 1917–19).
9. Robert W. Smuts, *Women and Work in America* (New York, 1959).
10. Kate Hevner Mueller, *Educating Women for a Changing World* (Minneapolis, 1954).
11. George D. Stoddard, *On the Education of Women* (New York, 1950).
12. Mirra Komarovsky, *Women in the Modern World* (Boston, 1953).
13. Abram Kardiner, *Sex and Morality* (Indianapolis, 1954).
14. Margaret Mead, *Male and Female* (New York, 1949).
See also:
Mary Beard, *A Changing Political Economy as it Affects Women* (Washington, 1934); *Women as a Force in History: A Study in Traditions and Realities* (New York, 1946).
Alva Myrdal, *Nation and Family* (New York and London, 1941).

NINE: ASCENT OF WOMAN: CRUISING ALTITUDE

1. Alva Myrdal, Address to Association of All-Ceylon's Women's Conference on Education for Citizenship, in Colombo, 1960 (unpublished).
2. Sam Waagenar, *Women of Israel* (London, 1961).
3. Georges Douart, *Du Kolkhoze au Kibboutz* (Paris, 1961).
4. Henrik F. Infield, *Utopia and Experiment* (New York, 1955).
5. Melford E. Spiro, *Kibbutz, Venture in Utopia* (Cambridge, Mass., 1956).
6. Georges Douart, *op. cit.*
7. L. F. Rushbrook Williams, *The State of Israel* (London, 1959).
8. Sulamith Schwartz Nardi, "Women in Israel," *Israel Today* No. 13 (Jerusalem, 1960).

9. *International Seminar on the Role of Women in a Developing Society* (Jerusalem, 1961).

10. Melford Spiro, *op. cit.*

11. Nicholas Dewitt, *Education and Professional Employment in the USSR* (Washington, 1962).

12. Paolo Robotti, *Nell' Unione Sovietica si vive cosi* (Rome, 1950).

13. International Union of Students, *21 Unforgettable Days in the Soviet Union* (Prague, 1950).

14. Nicholas Dewitt, *op. cit.*

15. Esther Peterson, "American Women at Work," *The American Review* (Bologna, 1961).

16. International Union of Students, *op. cit.*

17. William Benton, *This is the Challenge* (New York, 1958).

18. Arthur Koestler, *The Lotos and the Robot* (New York, 1961).

19. Simone de Beauvoir, *La longue marche* (Paris, 1957).

20. Gaetano Tumiati, *Buongiorno Cina* (Milan-Rome, 1954).

21. Il Ponte, *La Cina d'oggi* (Florence, 1958).

22. Ruth Frances Woodsmall, *Women and the New East* (Washington, 1960).

23. Philip M. Hauser, *Population and World Politics* (Glencoe, Ill., 1958).

See also:

Aleksandr Birman, *Oltre la retribuzione* (Rome, 1961).

Oriana Fallaci, *Il Sesso Inutile* (Milan, 1961).

John Gunther, *Inside Russia Today* (New York, 1958).

Il Ponte, *Israele* (Florence, 1956).

M. Strouve, *U.S.S.R. Faits et Chiffres* (Moscow, 1957).

EPILOGUE: MY OWN UTOPIA

1. St. Augustine, *The City of God.*

2. St. Clemens Romanus, in *The Apostolic Fathers,* L. B. Lightfoot, ed. (London, 1890).

3. H. J. Muller, from address on 100th anniversary of the publication of Darwin's *Origin of the Species* (University of Indiana, November 29, 1959).

4. John B. S. Haldane, *Daedalus, or Science and the Future* (London, 1924).

5. For cultural determination of sex, see Ashley Montagu, *Man In Process* (New York, 1962).

6. Julian Huxley, "Culture and Evolution," in Roe and Simpson, *Behavior and Evolution* (New Haven, 1958).

7. Havelock Ellis, *Man and Woman* (London, 1930).

8. Florida Scott-Maxwell, *Women and Sometimes Men* (New York, 1961).

9. Oriana Fallaci, *Il Sesso Inutile* (Milan, 1961).

10. Lewis M. Terman and Catherine Cox Miles, *Personality Studies in Masculinity and Femininity* (New York-London, 1936).

11. Viola Klein, *The Feminine Character* (London, 1946).

12. Jules and Edmond Goncourt, *The Woman of the Eighteenth Century: Her Life from Birth to Death, Her Love and Her Philosophy in the World of Salon, Shop, and Street* (New York, 1927).

Index

INDEX

243

Date Due